NON MINIMA SED MAXIMA PETIMUS

Newton Aycliffe

A Long History of a New Town

Stephen Creaney

Printed in Great Britain by Newton Press, Blue Bridge Centre
St. Cuthberts Way, Newton Aycliffe, Co. Durham, DL5 6DS

This edition produced by Mandy Bloom Memoirs:
www.mandybloom.co.uk

ISBN: 9781527257443

Inside Front Cover:

The Heraldic Shield has a background of red surrounded by a border in *or* (gold) representing the boundaries of the designated site of the new town of Newton Aycliffe. The Chevron across the shield is in *argent* (silver) and is an allusion to the bridge over St. Cuthbert's Way, linking the town with Aycliffe Industrial Park. The sheaves of corn forming the garbs in the shield are taken from the Arms of the Eden Family, of whose estate the site of the new town formed a part, and the hand grenade on the chevron represents the Royal Ordnance Factory, out of which the Industrial Park was converted.

The supporters in *argent* are the Lions Rampant in the Arms of the See of Durham, differenced with mail gauntlets in allusion to the military activities of the Bishops of Durham and holding Crosses Pattonce in allusion to the old form of the Arms of the See.

The Crest consists of an oak tree on a limestone cliff surmounting a helm. The oak tree is a reference to the forests which formerly covered this part of the country, from which was taken the Saxon name 'acle' meaning 'oak leaf', from which the name of Aycliffe was derived. One of the branches of the oak tree is broken and bent down to indicate the disappearance from the area of its oak forests and with a lesser branch the letter 'A', thus forming a rebus on Aycliffe.

The motto reads: 'Not the least but the greatest we seek'

The grant of Arms to the Aycliffe Development Corporation was made by the College of Heralds in October 1956, and later transferred to the Town Council.

Dedication

To my parents who spent their adult lives as pioneers
and then long-term residents of Newton Aycliffe:

James Grant Creaney 1925 – 1995
(Lived in Newton Aycliffe 1948 – 1995)

Eva Creaney 1924 – 2012
(Lived in Newton Aycliffe 1948 – 2012)

Newton Aycliffe's iconic 'Blue Bridge' looking north into the town – as it is today

As built in 1956 to link the New Town to the Industrial Estate and carry the Clarence Railway over St. Cuthbert's Way.

Contents

About the Author
Stephen Creaney

I was born in 1952 to parents Eva and Jim Creaney who were living in a Prefab at 15, Clarence Green, Newton Aycliffe. Eva and Jim were original pioneers, having occupied their Prefab in December 1948. We moved across Clarence Green to 20, Clarence Chare in the summer of 1953 and were its second occupants.

I attended Sugar Hill Primary School until July 1964 and then went to Ferryhill Grammar Technical School until 1971. I followed this by attending Durham University (1971 – 1974) and Newcastle University (1974 – 1977). Thirty-eight years working in the oil industry around the world followed until retirement to Somerset in 2015. I left Newton Aycliffe in late 1977, but have returned every year since to visit parents and relatives.

I compiled this book as a way of 'giving back' to the town I grew up in. Sales proceeds will be donated to a Newton Aycliffe charity.

The author aged 8, c.1960 sitting on a Clarence Chare road sign. The original Prefabs are in the background, an original light pole is shown and notice the seat on Clarence Green has already been vandalised - author not responsible!

Right: Stephen Creaney pictured in 2019

Foreword

Newton Aycliffe passed its seventieth birthday last year. The town has grown and developed, decade-by-decade, since the days of its earliest pioneers, and matured into the modern and vibrant community we see today. The original Beveridge vision of a town with abundant open spaces and green areas has been realised and today both residents and visitors appreciate and enjoy its pleasant environment. This book is a fascinating study of the development of the town, full of anecdotes, photographs and memories, particularly of its first few decades. It will appeal to long-time residents of Newton Aycliffe, but also to newcomers, who will gain an insight into the people and events which have shaped the community, which I am proud to serve as Mayor.

Councillor Mrs. Mary Dalton
Mayor of Great Aycliffe

Introduction

Lord William Beveridge described Newton Aycliffe in a Coronation Souvenir booklet (1953) as follows: 'We are a New Town, the newest in one way of all the New Towns because we are being built where before there was practically no population and no building. We do not, as many of our fellow New Towns do, incorporate a smaller old town or have in our area or near it people already settled there. Yet while we are so completely without a past in the place where we live, we do not want to forget the past'

In 2017 Newton Aycliffe celebrated the 70th anniversary of its designation as a New Town. 2018 was the 70th anniversary of building commencing and of the first residents moving in.

There has been some confusion related to anniversary dates – other new towns such as Stevenage, Harlow etc. celebrate their Designation Date (the date that the Government commissioned the individual town). In this case 1947 would be the celebration year for Newton Aycliffe. However, Newton Aycliffe has historically celebrated the year of the sod cutting ceremony and the dedication of the first house (1948) – the 25th anniversary was in 1973 and the 50th anniversary was in 1998. Even the first anniversary party was held on November 9th, 1949 at the Gretna Green Wedding Inn on the Great North Road (A1) east of the town.

A number of people have suggested that the time is right to produce a book on the history of Newton Aycliffe. The following is a quote from 'The Newton News' website (The local online newsletter for Newton Aycliffe): *'There is no adequate history of Newton Aycliffe.'* The purpose of this book is to modestly try and fill this gap in the 'popular' literature documenting the earliest history of this 'not so old' New Town. This is also an attempt to capture the slowly eroding knowledge and memories of the generation who occupied Newton Aycliffe in the 1950s and 1960s. In addition, the opportunity has been taken to document the history of this part of Great Aycliffe prior to the initiation of Newton Aycliffe – an aspect not reported in much detail elsewhere.

The first homes to be occupied in Newton Aycliffe were 41 hastily erected, prefabricated bungalows. These original occupants lived in a mud laden building site without facilities. Remarkably the generation of 'Pioneers' who first occupied Newton Aycliffe as adults are now either in their 90s, or may have passed away, whilst others may have relocated outside the area in the intervening years. It is unknown if any of these original adult occupants of the 41 pre-fabs are still available for primary source recollections. Many of their children are available and some have been consulted. The 'Photographic History of Newton Aycliffe' Group on Facebook has been an excellent source of anecdotal information from both long time residents and former residents of the town.

A number of more academic studies have described elements of the grand social experiment that the post-war new towns represented but few described this social experiment within the context of daily life in Newton Aycliffe.

The structure of this book begins with chapters that cover broad periods of time prior to the creation of Newton Aycliffe. It then covers the early pioneering years on a year-by-year basis as physical construction and social development proceeded rapidly. From the later 1960s the chapters focus on a decade at a time with the post-millennium years grouped as a single chapter. An attempt has been made to present information in chronological order where possible within each chapter.

Appendices have been used to present some basic information.

Acknowledgements

I would like to thank Councillor Mrs. Mary Dalton, Mayor of Great Aycliffe who provided the foreword for this book and Amanda Donald and the staff at Great Aycliffe Town Council for access to their files of historic photographs.

Many other people have assisted with the compilation of this book directly or indirectly: The staff at the London School of Economics facilitated access to Lord Beveridge's archive.

The staff at the National Archive held at Swindon assisted with access to the Windlestone Estate Sale documents as part of the Eden Archive.

The staff at Durham County Records Office was very helpful with access permission to use photographs in their collection.

'The Newtonian'/'Newton News' is a remarkable archive of events in Newton Aycliffe and the online archive of back issues is a crucial historic set of documents. I would like to personally thank the Howarth family for their dedication to this archive.

Vivien and David Ellis have been collecting historical data for the Great Aycliffe area for many years and are acknowledged here for their help with the preparation of this book.

One particular book written by Vera Chapman (1995) is singled out as a substantial documentation of life in Newton Aycliffe through photographs. The photographs she compiled are an extremely comprehensive contribution to the history of Newton Aycliffe. Vera passed away in July 2015 and her contribution to local history is acknowledged here.

A number of online sites contain short histories of Newton Aycliffe and/or a number of photographs from the early years of the towns' history. These have been leveraged as much as possible. A number of these are a little uncertain about event dates and this aspect has been checked using back copies of 'The Newtonian' as well as Corporation and Community Association annual reports. These online sources include:

The Great Aycliffe Town Council for the photo inventory on their website, The Aycliffe Village Local History website and particularly David and Vivien Ellis, The Arun M. Chandran website archive and Archive photos from 'The Newton News'. The most comprehensive single review of Newton Aycliffe total history is likely the short town history article on 'The Newton News' web page authored by Councillor John D. Clare. In July / August 2019, 'The Newton News' published a seven-part History of Newton Aycliffe by Councillor John D. Clare that provided a view of Newton Aycliffe from pre-Roman times to present.

In addition, all those residents and former residents who contribute to the Facebook group 'A Photographic History of Newton Aycliffe' are acknowledged for their very diverse memories. From this group I would specifically like to thank the late David Charlesworth for access to his well-preserved collection of early Newton Aycliffe 'artefacts' (now in the possession of Great Aycliffe Town Council); Desnee Charlton for allowing the use of a personal family photograph; Ian Robertson / Ernest Stanley for the Cobbler's Hall photo; Andrew Sayer for the Clarence Railway / A1 junction photo; and Geoff Bilton for access to his late father's photographs.

I would also like to thank Mandy Bloom who produced the final print version of this book and coordinated all aspects of its publication.

The book was printed by the Newton Press and I would like to thank Stuart Howarth for his advice throughout the process.

Every attempt has been made to adhere to copyright legislation and to receive permission to use material from others. My apologies to anyone who I was unable to contact.

I would like to thank my family for enduring what became an obsession for several months.

Stephen Creaney
2020

List of Figures

Figures in Appendices

Chapter One

Rural Great Aycliffe - Before 1825

Although Newton Aycliffe only appeared as an entity in 1948 it is, like most places, located in an area with a much longer history. Iron Age roundhouse archaeology was discovered during excavations for the Hitachi Factory as recently as 2013/2014. The northeast has a rich Roman history with the Vinovium site being a few miles away at Bishop Auckland. Clare (2019) has suggested that Burn Lane was a Roman road, which seems a reasonable hypothesis. This earlier history all built towards the establishment of Newton Aycliffe; it affected its ultimate boundaries and even some of the names of its areas and roads.

The natural landscape that would become Newton Aycliffe has East Durham's characteristic Permian Magnesian Limestone as its foundation. These rocks are about 240 million years old. This is actually the yellow dolomite seen in road cuts and numerous quarries throughout the northeast (including those around Aycliffe Village). It provides a generally alkaline, somewhat impoverished soil.

The much more recent glaciations (the latest being about 14 thousand years old) produced a generally flat topography, covered in boulder clay, that is often boggy. As the glaciers receded they left large glacial lakes across County Durham and in these lakes thick, clay-rich sediments were deposited. As these lakes were filled up the residual drainage was via the small streams (including Woodham Burn, Demon's Beck etc.) and ditches we see today that ultimately drain into the meandering River Skerne.

Prior to the industrialisation of this part of County Durham these were clean rivers and streams and linen was produced throughout the Skerne drainage area. The Skerne operated a number of water mills along its length including a corn mill at Ricknall (east of present day Newton Aycliffe) and mills in Aycliffe Village and Brafferton. Small quarries into the Magnesian Limestone have been used for local building stone – examples occur along the Woodham Burn and at Bluebell Wood as well as the more massive operations around Aycliffe Village. Many of the local farmhouses were built from this Magnesian Limestone. Great Aycliffe is south of the geologic subcrop of the Carboniferous coal measures beneath the Permian Magnesian Limestone and therefore coal is absent in the area. This is why the Great Aycliffe area remained rural throughout the time that most of the area to the west was heavily mined for coal.

The position of Great Aycliffe on the Great North Road between Durham and York probably exposed it to the passage of many troops as Scots fought English over the centuries. Little specific documentation exists of the impact on Aycliffe but the impact on local farms and villages can be imagined.

There are three much older communities that surround and enclose modern Newton Aycliffe. These are Aycliffe Village (actually called just Aycliffe until Newton Aycliffe was contemplated), School Aycliffe and Woodham. All have a significant presence for centuries before 1948. Across this time the term 'Aycliffe' appears as Acle, Acley, Ackham, Aikcliffe and Aikeliffe.

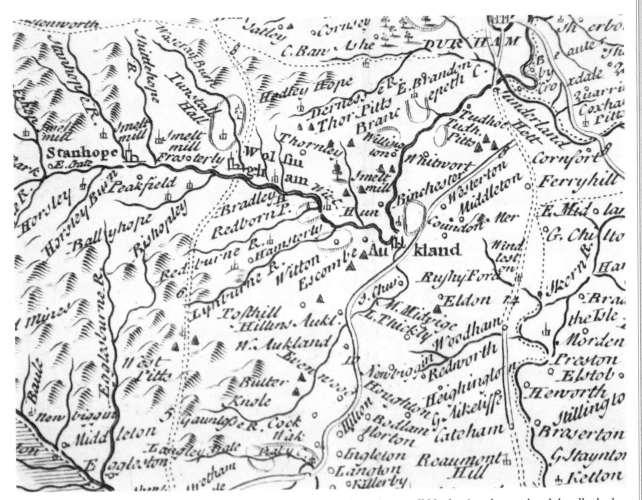

Figure 1 - An excerpt from the County Durham map of Rocque (1753) – small black triangles are local, landlocked coalmines – the entire output of which would be moved by packhorses through local lanes. Map from personal collection.

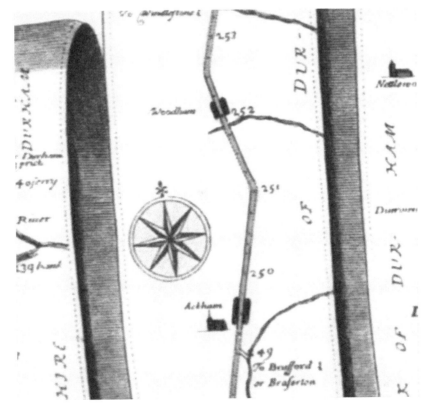

Figure 2 - A section of Ogilby's Strip Map (1675) – Map from personal collection.

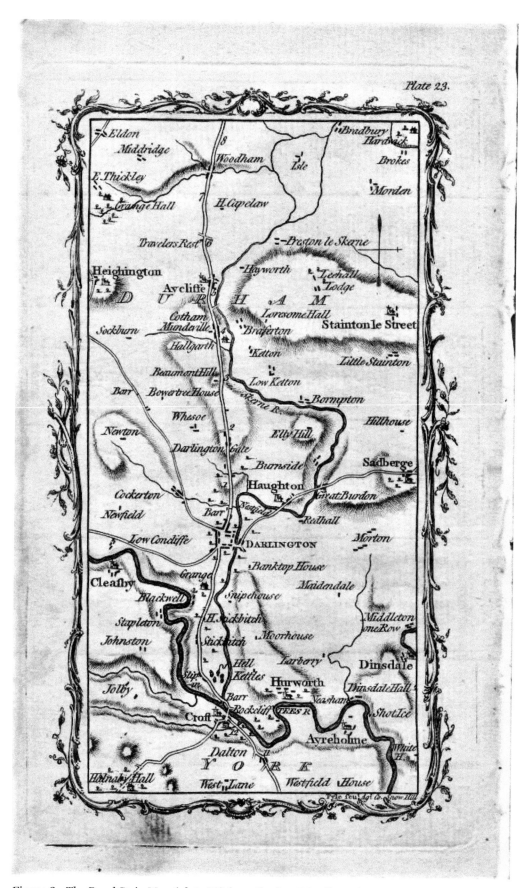

Figure 3 - The Road Strip Map (plate 23) from Croft to Woodham (Mostyn, 1776) The first appearance of the Travellers' Rest on a map of the Great North Road. Map from personal collection.

The modern term 'Aycliffe' was first used by Mostyn in 1776 (shown in Figure 3). In general the term Acle was used on maps until about 1720, Akham and Aikeliffe variants were used until about 1790 and after that the term Aycliffe comes into common usage. Aycliffe Village dates from Saxon time with St. Andrew's Church having Saxon crosses in the churchyard.

The name Aycliffe and its precursors apparently derive from the Saxon terms for a 'clearing in an oak forest'. School Aycliffe probably got its name from a Viking occupant rather than any historic association with schools. School Aycliffe contains two Grade II listed buildings 1) Old Farm Cottage and one gable wall from the cottage dates to the 16th century (according to the listing) and 2) The nurses teaching centre which dates to 1835. Woodham has a series of earth works that record a medieval village that was later abandoned. According to the Aycliffe Village website Saxon artefacts were also found on the site of Woodham.

There is much to be learned from older maps of County Durham. Possibly the earliest map of County Durham is that of Rudd in 1569. It shows Aycliffe Village (Acle), School Aycliffe (Scole Acle) and Woodham (Werdham). The subsequent map of County Durham produced by Christopher Saxton in 1579 also shows Aycliffe Village and School Aycliffe but Woodham is absent. These earliest maps all highlight a dominant lane / track that will ultimately become the Great North Road. It runs north to south from Yorkshire through County Durham, linking York – Darlington – Durham and Newcastle.

Additional 17th century maps of County Durham are essentially copies of Saxton's work with no new surveying. These countywide maps are large scale showing villages and significant manor houses but rarely show minor farms. They imply that there are no farms etc. between these villages but this is likely a matter of scale or simply surveyor's omission. Figure 1 is one of the better quality maps produced in the mid 18th century. (Rocque, 1753)

In 1675 Ogilby produced the first 'strip map' series of the UK. These maps focused on single roads and showed communities on that road. The Darlington to Durham segment of the Great North Road map (Figure 2) shows Aycliffe Village (called Ackham) and Woodham. School Aycliffe is out of scope for this map and even at this scale any local farms are omitted. To the South of Figure 2 it does show the junction of a minor road at Harrogate Hill north of Darlington (actually where the White Horse stands today) with the annotation 'To the Cole Pitts', a reference to the packhorse traffic from coalmines west of Bishop Auckland.

The Great North Road was a major connective artery for road traffic and its development provided part of the foundation for Newton Aycliffe. It probably began as nothing more than a track connecting towns and villages of material size (Cooper, 2013). It may not have begun as a Roman road in the Aycliffe area – the major Roman road crossed the Tees at Piercebridge and passed through Vinovium (near Bishop Auckland) heading towards Hadrian's Wall. The early maps that show the Great North Road often have significant parts of it in 'dotted' lines, suggesting a temporary, infrequently used road surface. The line of the Great North Road follows the higher ground west of the former glacial lake that occupied the area of 'Carrs' (boggy, fenland) around Bradbury and Morden.

Figure 4 - The Travellers' Rest – A Complex of Farm Buildings, Cottages and The Bay Horse Inn (Photo from The Windlestone Estate Auction Papers, 1936)

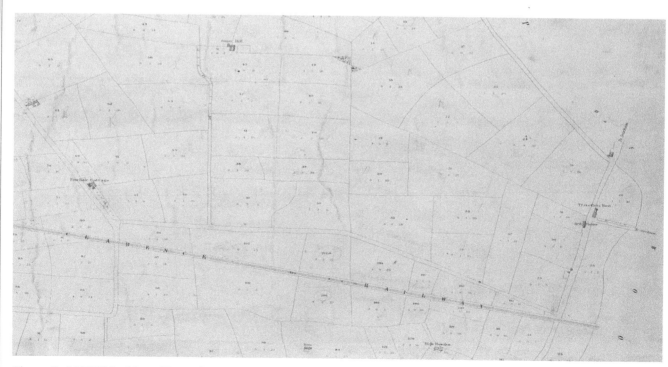

Figure 5 - 1838 Tithe Map of Part of Great Aycliffe Township (underlying map image with permission of Durham County Records Office)

Throughout the 18th century the Great North Road saw increasing 'Post Road' traffic as travel across the UK increased. This traffic was delivering long distance mail as well as transporting passengers. The horse drawn coaches required many facilities for both horses and humans. These occurred as Post Inns at Aycliffe Village, Travellers' Rest (near where the Gretna stands today), Woodham, and Rushyford in the Great Aycliffe area. The number of horses involved must have been significant as crews were exchanged when tired etc. Therefore a series of associated industries probably occurred including blacksmiths, stabling, farriers etc. These ancillary industries would also help whatever local farmers were in the area since all motive power at the farm would have been by horse or pony.

Additional horse traffic may have been provided by packhorses carrying coal from the area to the west. This is somewhat speculative but it is known that prior to the Stockton and Darlington Railway relatively small mines were worked in the Eldon, Shildon, Bishop Auckland, Coundon and Cockfield Fell areas. It seems likely that the movement of this coal from mine to market (Richmond, Darlington and the mouth of the Tees for export) may have utilised the lanes that cross the Great Aycliffe area (Burn Lane and New Lane). The numbers of packhorses involved could have been quite large – a single miner could hew up to 3 tons per day and a packhorse could carry about 2 cwt. Therefore 30 packhorses would be required to serve a single miners daily production!

The Travellers' Rest doesn't appear on a map until the road strip map of Mostyn (1776) (Figure 3) and is absent on earlier maps including several from the 1760s. Speculation would suggest the Travellers' Rest was built around 1770. Interestingly on the 1838 Tithe Map the Travellers' Rest is referred to as Red House (see Figure 5).

Interestingly the Travellers' Rest on Mostyn's map is shown at a significant intersection that was between New Lane, Burn Lane and the Great North Road. The photograph in Figure 4 shows the Bay Horse Inn (on the right end of the terrace) that was closed as an inn at the time of the photograph but still retains its odd pub sign (between the two upstairs windows). The 1856 Ordnance Survey map refers to the building in the location of the Gretna as the Traveller's Rest as does the 1838 Tithe map, however the 1851 census does call it the Gretna Green Inn with a Sarah Munby as the innkeeper. A speculation would suggest that all buildings around that junction were referred to as the Travellers' Rest that included the Bay Horse Inn and the Gretna Green Inn as early as 1851. This is supported by the 1841 census that lists two publicans resident at The Travellers' Rest with no mention of the Gretna Green Inn.

Note the nature of The Great North Road – a single carriageway with no centre line. It is the main north – south highway in the UK in the 1930s, an era with relatively limited vehicle traffic compared to today.

High Travellers' Rest is a series of four terraced cottages that were at the intersection of Burn Lane and the Great North Road. Chapman (1995) points out that three of the cottages were built of local magnesian limestone and the fourth was built of sandstone. This latter presumably was transported from the coal measures to the west and may have been built at a different time to the other three.

An inscription on a gravestone in Aycliffe Village church refers to the deaths of Ann and John Greeveson of Aycliffe Moor House who died in 1795 and 1796 respectively and this may refer to the Moor House shown in Figure 6.

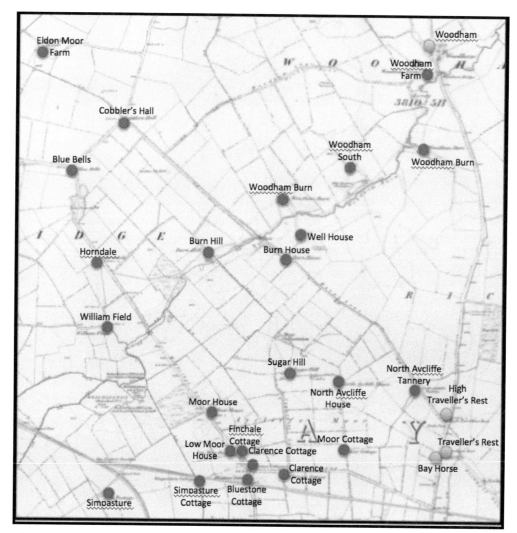

Figure 6 - 1856 1st Series Ordnance Survey Map – farms and cottages shown in red, Great North Road related inns and cottages in blue. Reproduced under a Creative Commons Attribution-NonCommercial-ShareAlike 4.0 International (CC-BY-NC-SA) licence with the permission of the National Library of Scotland.

Chapter Two

The Railway Era (1825 – 1939)

The coming of the railway to the Great Aycliffe area brought a number of significant changes to an otherwise rural setting. The Stockton and Darlington Railway (S&DR) was in place by 1825 – Locomotion No. 1 was in fact placed on the track at Heighington Station for the first time. This will have immediately curtailed all coal packhorse traffic through adjacent country lanes as all coal was now evacuated via the S&DR. In 1833 the Clarence Railway opened connecting these same coal mines more directly to Hartlepool, however onerous tariffs imposed by the S&DR to transport coal to Simpasture over their rails reduced its profitability.

By 1844 the Newcastle and Darlington Junction Railway (precursor to the East Coast Mainline) had been constructed and would have begun to diminish horse drawn traffic on the Great North Road. The Post Inns would have seen a reduction in trade as passengers and mail transferred to the railways.

The railways did bring a certain amount of local employment with the 19th century census data describing a number of local cottages (particularly in the Simpasture area) being occupied by railway workers with varying jobs (labourers, engine men, ticket master, gate men etc.).

The oldest map with enough detail to see individual buildings is the Great Aycliffe Tithe map of 1838. These maps were created in response to the Tithe Commutation Act of 1836 and were to establish how many habitations needed to pay tithes (in the form of cash instead of a proportion of crops etc.). The area that was to become Newton Aycliffe has a small number of farms and a few buildings associated with the Great North Road.

The Tithe map was being surveyed at the time the Clarence Railway was just opening which likely explains why no railway cottages or infrastructure appear on the map.

The first series of Ordnance Survey maps were published in 1856 and provide the earliest comprehensive and detailed look at the area that will become Newton Aycliffe. Figure 6 shows the 1856 First Series OS map (6" to the mile) with farms, inns etc. highlighted. There is clearly a cluster of additional cottages around the Clarence Railway (generally in the Simpasture area) for railway support workers. An apparently 'new' farm has appeared since 1838 – North Aycliffe House as well as a 'new' business – North Aycliffe Tannery. The Coulson family were long-term residents at North Aycliffe House and also operated the Tannery. The Tannery was sited on Burn Lane (now Moore Lane) almost exactly where the present sports club stands. An anecdote on the Aycliffe Village local history website describes the discovery of a 'pit' of animal bones on Moore Lane during road construction – almost certainly a remnant of the Tannery.

Little had changed through the First World War as reflected by the 1923 3rd Series Ordnance Survey map (6" to the mile). (Figure 7) The only obvious change is the apparent abandonment of the North Aycliffe Tannery. Checking the 19th century census data the Tannery apparently ceases to operate by 1891 and no one locally claims to be a Tanner after this.

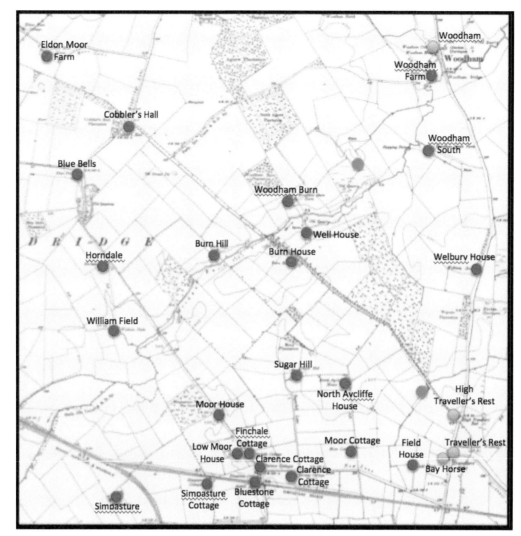

Figure 7 - 1923 3ʳᵈ Series Ordnance Survey map with farms etc. highlighted in red, Great North Road related buildings in blue and abandoned buildings in grey. Reproduced under a Creative Commons Attribution-NonCommercial-ShareAlike 4.0 International (CC-BY-NC-SA) licence with the permission of the National Library of Scotland.

The Clarence Railway itself underwent significant change in 1913 when the North Eastern Railway chose to electrify the line between Shildon and Newport in Teesside, possibly as a precursor to electrifying the whole East Coast Mainline. The line began running in 1916 and although the electrification was costly (£200,000) it only lasted until 1936/1937. Ten electric locomotives were built, as well as two generator buildings – one at Preston-le-Skerne (behind the Blacksmiths Arms pub) that was ultimately demolished in the 1960s.

Figure 8 is a rare photograph of the Travellers' Rest junction in the 1930s showing the overhead electrical equipment as well as the signal box at the junction of the Great North Road (A1) and the Clarence Railway. This photo is taken from approximately the subsequent location of the A167 bridge that is there today.

Figure 8 – Rare grainy photograph of the Traveller's Rest junction of the Clarence Railway and the Great North Road (therefore pre-1941). Note the overhead electrification (photo provided with permission by Andrew Sayer)

In 1936 the Aycliffe Mental Deficiency Colony was built in nearby School Aycliffe. Today the name sounds very 'politically incorrect' and certainly by the 1950s it was simply referred to as Aycliffe Hospital. This was 'an institution of its time' when people with various, non-violent disabilities were institutionalised. The attitude of the day was to remove people from society, thankfully one that has changed with the much more progressive treatment of such illnesses. One Newton Aycliffe connected celebrity – Mark Gatiss (a comedian who attended Woodham Comprehensive School and developed and acted in The League of Gentlemen) lived in Heighington / School Aycliffe and had a summer job as a gardener at the Hospital. Both his parents worked at the facility. He describes finding an old sign while weeding, describing 'Aycliffe Colony for the Mentally Defective'. He also described Newton Aycliffe itself as 'a grim post-industrial town' (Interview in The Guardian online, 2004).

Another significant event which took place in 1936 provides considerable insight into the buildings in existence prior to the development of Newton Aycliffe. The Eden Estate (centred on Windlestone Hall west of Rushyford) was in extreme financial difficulty and Sir Timothy Eden needed to auction off a portion of the estate to pay death duties. The auction brochure provides a complete description of every property and photographs of some. Additionally maps showing the extent of land associated with each property are provided (see Figure 9). These descriptions have been transcribed here as Appendix 1. The sale took place on Thursday, 12th November 1936 at the King's Head Hotel, Darlington. As a matter of interest, the famous Jarrow March would have been progressing down the Great North Road through Great Aycliffe in the same month as this sale, indicative of the desperately difficult economic conditions for working people in the coalfields of Northern England in the 1930s.

It is hard to comprehend the fate of the sitting tenants as this sale occurred, some bought their tenant farms and others had to relocate. None of these people yet anticipated the coming compulsory purchase that would occur when Newton Aycliffe was designated in 1947.

In a rather delightful book entitled 'Far Off Bell' Gladys O'Connor (nee Wheldon) describes her early years living at Greenfield Farm and attending school in Middridge. The book is semi-fictionalised but still reflects a somewhat bucolic existence in Great Aycliffe in the early 20th century.

Figure 9 - Partial Property map of the Windlestone Estate from the sale documents of 1936. All coloured areas were lots that were put up for sale. Numbers in circles correspond to lot numbers in Appendix One.

To the degree possible, Appendix 1 provides an inventory of the houses present on the site of Newton Aycliffe prior to 1948 as well as photographs if available. The data from the Windlestone sale document has been supplemented with additional photographs where available, many from Chapman (1995). Appendix 3 includes an inventory of residents of Newton Aycliffe in 1951 and amongst these are residents of the farms and cottages not yet demolished. Figure 10 provides an indication of where these farms, cottages and houses were by plotting them on a modern satellite image of Newton Aycliffe.

Figure 10 - Locations of older farms, cottages and houses (mostly now demolished) plotted on a modern satellite image of Newton Aycliffe. Farms and cottages shown in red, Great North Road related inns and cottages in blue

In this early period a Methodist Church was opened adjacent to Low Moor Farm (close to the modern Simpasture Gate shops) – it was initially in a disused railway carriage. In 1929 a new wooden building was opened to replace the carriage. A sketch of the new structure appeared in the brochure associated with the opening of the new Methodist Church in 1959 (Figure 11) and a photo from Chapman (1995) is shown in Figure 12. The Church also appears in the background in Figure 65.

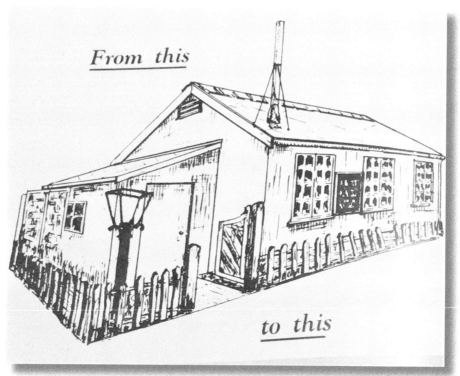

Figure 11 - Sketch of the earliest church (Methodist) in the Newton Aycliffe area. Constructed in 1929. The sketch is taken from the program for the opening of the new Methodist Church at Neville Parade

Figure 12 - Photograph of the Original Methodist Chapel in Newton Aycliffe. (From Chapman, 1995)

In December 1968, 'The Newtonian' interviewed original Simpasture resident Lillian Holmes. At the time of the interview, Lillian lived at 14, Church Close and her mother Laura Stevens lived at 18, Church Close. Laura had lived on Woodham Grange Farm when she married in 1918, but soon left to live in Bishop Auckland. They then returned to live in Clarence House at Simpasture Gate, where Lillian was born in 1930. Lillian gave an evocative account of life in the 'village' of Simpasture; cycling down New Lane to the A1 to get the bus to school; and Methodist Circuit rallies where all local residents would gather – all very bucolic. She was baptised in the former railway carriage that served as the Methodist Church before the present church. She recalled little contact with workers from the Ordnance Factory during the war since buses and trains brought them all in. After the war she recalled Prefabs being brought in by lorry and placed in Clarence Green and Travellers' Green.

Woodham Village was a medieval village of some size – this medieval village is now represented by hummocky landscape on the east side of the Great North Road. It has been described anecdotally as having been destroyed by marauding Scots and therefore abandoned.

In the 1841 census a community of 52 individuals lived in Woodham and related farms. This had dropped to 41 by 1861. Most were farmers or farm labourers with a blacksmith and a publican. The 1856 and 1923 Ordnance survey maps show a marked contrast in buildings on the east side of the Great North Road (Figure 13). This seems to be describing a slowly dying farming community.

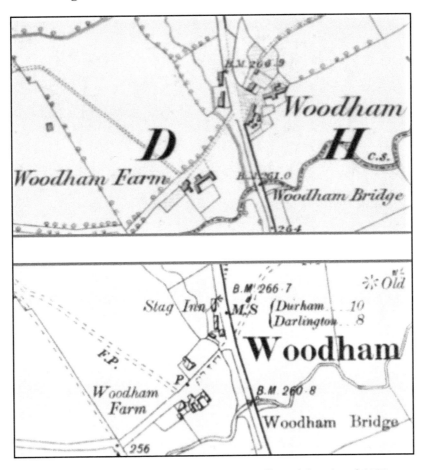

Figure 13 - 1856 Ordnance Survey map of Woodham (above) and 1923 map (below). Note the buildings on the east side of the Great North Road in 1856 that are gone in 1923. Reproduced under a Creative Commons Attribution-NonCommercial-ShareAlike 4.0 International (CC-BY-NC-SA) licence with the permission of the National Library of Scotland.

The inn at Woodham was probably related to both the early population of the village as well as passing post road trade on the Great North Road. The inn was variously called 'The Rising Stag', 'The Buck Inn' or 'The Stag Inn' in 19th century census data and on Ordnance Survey maps. The inn no longer existed according to the 1936 Windlestone Estate auction brochure however the brochure describes Woodham House as having a bar with a taproom at the rear! Obviously from a previous life as 'The Stag Inn'.

The houses shown in Figure 14 at Woodham in 1936 are virtually unchanged in outward appearance at the present day. See Figure 114.

Figure 14 - Woodham House (on the left) – probably formerly "The Rising Stag Inn". (Photo taken in 1936 and from the Windlestone Estate Sale papers)

Chapter Three

The area during World War II (1939 – 1945)

The Second World War brought extreme change to the Great Aycliffe area. Much has been written about the munitions works that were built south of the Clarence Railway. Royal Ordnance Factory 59 (Filling Factory 8) commenced operations in the spring of 1941 and had cost £7 million to build. The factory filled shell casings largely produced at an ordnance factory at Spennymoor. Beginning in May 1940 approximately 1000 buildings were constructed, disguised and commissioned with between 16,000 to 25,000 local employees (mostly women – called 'Aycliffe Angels' after the Nazi propagandist traitor William Joyce aka 'Lord Haw Haw' referred to them as 'the Angels of Aycliffe' in a radio broadcast).

The siting of R.O.F. 59 was based on a number of factors: it is in the north (reduced likelihood of bombing), there were very strong rail connections via the S&DR as well as the Clarence Railway and strong road connections via the Great North Road. A large underutilised work force of miner's wives was also locally available.

The site, at the time, was quite isolated likely minimising damage if a significant accident occurred. Even the foggy weather tendency of the local area has been cited as a good reason to build a 'stealth' facility!

The buildings typically were single-storey, connected by many walkways and heated from two central boiler houses (which required 26 miles of insulated pipes which were quickly laid above ground and arched above the walkways). An eight-foot chain-linked fence, topped with barbed wire, surrounded the whole facility. In addition, the buildings were isolated from one another by earth embankments to minimise any damage should an accidental explosion occur in one unit and the walkways and factory floors themselves were coated in non-spark surfaces.

Accidents did occur and a number of deaths were recorded - their extent hopefully limited by these preventative measures. Figure 15 shows a series of typical views across the Ordnance Factory.

Figure 15 - Views across the ordnance factory.

Figure 16 – One of Two Centralised Boiler Houses for R.O.F. 59 – They provided heat to most of the Ordnance Factory. This one was located on the north of the site adjacent to the Clarence Railway. (Photo from Chapman, 1995)

As part of the construction process some 'adjustments' were required for the local infrastructure. Two large, new railway stations were built as shown on Figure 17. These were at Simpasture (Station 'A') to receive passengers from the Shildon – Bishop Auckland – Crook area and Demon's Bridge (Station 'B') that received workers from the east (Stockton etc.). The connection of Demon's Bridge station to the Clarence Railway created huge congestion since the Great North Road (A1) crossed the Clarence Railway with a simple, gated level crossing at that time (see Figure 8). To remedy this the line of the Great North Road was altered to rise up and over the Clarence Railway at the bridge that is there today. There was a slightly sad outcome of this needed adjustment – the new line of the A1 required the removal of the Travellers' Rest complex of buildings (Figure 18). The old line of the Great North Road is marked today by a caravan storage facility on the site. The site of Demon's Bridge railway station is now the Aycliffe Nature Park.

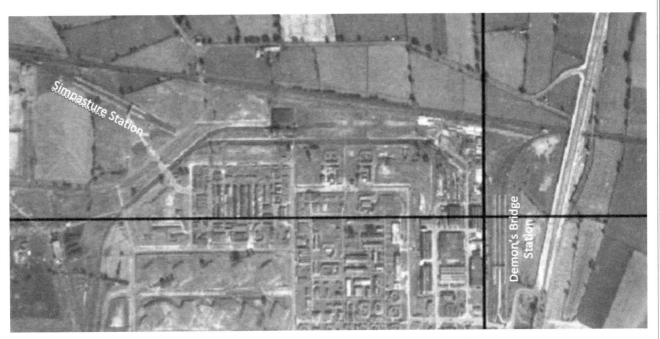

Figure 17 - 1940s Aerial Photograph showing R.O.F. 59 and the two new railway stations at Simpasture and Demons Bridge. (Underlying aerial photo from Durham County Record Office)

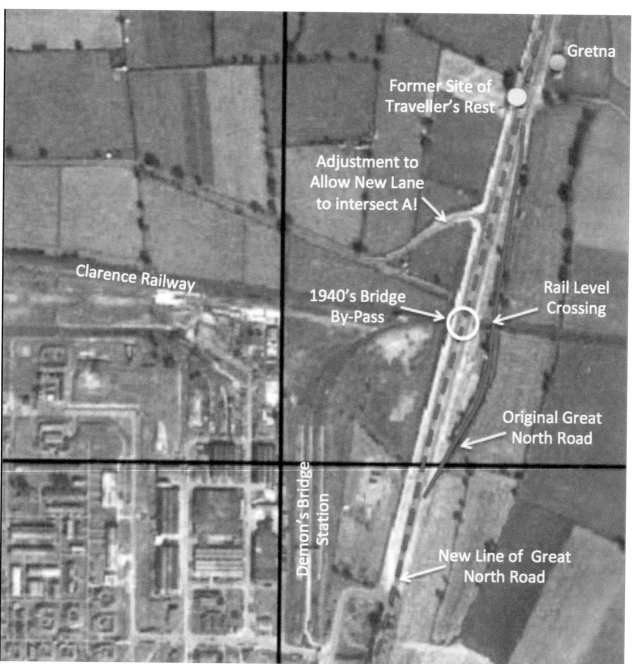

Figure 18 - 1940s Aerial Photo illustrating adjustments made to the Great North Road to accommodate the new station at Demon's Bridge. (Underlying aerial photo from Durham County Record Office)

On May 15th 1942 Prime Minister Winston Churchill visited R.O.F. 59 (Figure 19). Deputy Prime Minister Clement Atlee (to become Labour Prime Minister after the war) also attended – shown in Figure 19 behind Churchill (touching his hat). The figure to the far left is the ever-present Walter Henry Thompson who was Churchill's bodyguard throughout the war.

Figure 19 - Prime Minister Winston Churchill visits the munitions factory (R.O.F. 59).

Figure 20 - 1940s Aerial Photograph showing the Aycliffe Secure Centre under construction. (Underlying aerial photo from Durham County Record Office)

An often forgotten component of Newton Aycliffe was probably the first residential construction done in association with the 'New Town'. Aycliffe School (or Aycliffe Approved School and now known as Aycliffe Secure Centre) was built and opened in July 1942. It was initially built as a temporary hostel for munitions workers and the plasterboard construction soon got it christened 'cardboard city' by the subsequent child residents. (Figure 20)

As a resident of Newton Aycliffe in the 1950s it was a common sight to see young men clad in corduroy in two columns walking behind their schoolmaster. A brief reading of blogs associated with former residents of Aycliffe School suggests that some residents had a miserable time whereas others did better. Apparently it was better regarded than an alternate facility in Stanhope in Weardale.

The Aycliffe facility was the 'Classifying School' where incoming children were classified according to perceived intelligence, age, behaviour etc. (Gittins, 1952). The children were then placed into appropriate approved schools (so-called 'Teaching Schools'). The government report by Gittins (1952) presents a rather frightening picture of a 'big brother' approach to delinquency.

Around the periphery of R.O.F. 59 a number of additional buildings and other construction occurred. The area was generally surrounded by a series of 'pill boxes' (concrete defensive guard posts with gun 'slits' in the walls – see Figure 27). These were still present in the mid – late 1950s and provided a good play structure for local children!

A number of small houses were built on the western edge of Aycliffe Village to house critical ROF staff (Congreve Terrace, for example). In addition a number of buildings were constructed in the area that would become Barrington Road / Pease Way. These were administrative offices and would become the original Aycliffe Development Council offices in the post-war years as well as housing the R.A.F.A. Club.

There was also a gunnery range from that area northwest toward Woodham Burn, presumably for testing ordnance. There was a terminal earth bank beside Woodham Burn to restrict 'over shoot'. Many former resident children remember playing on 'The Ranges' near Woodham Burn in the 1950s. The Royal Ordnance Factory 59 closed in October 1945. By the end of the war it is estimated that R.O.F. 59 produced/filled over 700 million bullets plus other ordnance.

As a child in the 1950s there was still significant 'debris' from the ROF efforts to be found around the trading estate. Many old batteries, asbestos sheeting and, according to letters to the Aycliffe Development Corporation from September 1950 still some live ammunition!

Figure 21 - 1940s Air Photo highlighting WWII buildings in the future Barrington Road / Pease Way area as well as the ordnance testing range running toward Woodham Burn

1952 Air Photo showing perspective view of the same area. (Underlying aerial photo from Durham County Record Office)

Defective heating pipes   Engineer   Print Room   Boiler Room   Admin. Block

Board Room

Horticulture

Direct labour

Architects and Finance Depts.

Figure 22 - Newly converted WWII buildings at Barrington Road re-purposed as the first Aycliffe Development Corporation offices. (Photo from Durham County Records Office)

Figure 23 - Barrington Road WWII era buildings in Newton Aycliffe today (2018) – home of the R.A.F.A. Club and formerly Aycliffe Development Corporation Offices.

Figure 24 - Aycliffe Development Corporation Finance Department, July 1948. Posed outside their offices that will become the RAFA Club. Note overhead heating pipes in background. (From Chapman, 1995)

The work at R.O.F. 59 was so secret that very few photographs were permitted during wartime. A number of photographs of large groups of workers were taken after the war (Figure 25 is a typical example) but their dangerous work in support of the war effort went unrecognised for many years. In 1997 Councillor Tony Moore lobbied the new Prime Minister (Tony Blair) and a movement began to recognise the 'Angels'. In 2000 the local newspaper, 'The Northern Echo' continued the campaign for this recognition and eventually a memorial was placed near St. Clare's Church (see Figure 26). The Queen and Prime Minister Tony Blair attended the memorial service.

The 'pill box' shown in Figure 27 is actually from a site to the southwest of the modern trading estate where a number of storage bunkers still exist on farmland. They are used by the local farmer for storage. There were a number of them along the line of the Clarence Railway that children played on in the 1950s.

The outline of the Demon's Bridge railway station was still visible on aerial photographs as late as 1958 but was no longer present by the early 1960s where it was simply a muddy patch of ground adjacent to the Crowborough factory and south of the 'newt ponds' which would go on to be a Nature Preserve.

A comprehensive historic and photographic collection for Royal Ordnance Factory 59 is summarised at: http://www.communigate.co.uk/ne/aycliffeangels/index.phtml which is a website sponsored by Northumbria University.

Figure 25 - A typical 'Aycliffe Angels' group photograph from 1945. There are several photos taken in this location of groups, presumably in the same session.

Figure 26 - The Aycliffe Angels Memorial as it stands today (2018) at St. Clare's Church in Newton Aycliffe.

Figure 27 - A familiar site to many from the 1950s – these 'pill boxes' were built during WWII and surrounded the Royal Ordnance Factory. They were originally designed for armed defence.

43

Chapter Four

Newton Aycliffe - From Concept to Reality (1945 – 1948)

Lord William Beveridge can be considered the chief architect of the post war welfare state. He was a liberal economist who was the director of the London School of Economics until 1937 when he became Master of University College, Oxford. It was rumoured that his departure from the London School of Economics was related to his long held belief in the controversial subject of 'Eugenics'. This was a popular thesis in the early part of the 20th century and described a belief that selective breeding could increase the 'quality' of humanity. The worst manifestation of these beliefs occurred in Nazi Germany before and during the Second World War. This was a component of a generally held belief in a broader vision of social engineering that was manifest in the Garden Cities of the early 20th century (Welwyn Garden City and Letchworth being the earliest examples). The design concept of these Garden Cities was based on many green spaces (parks, greens etc.), large gardens and reduced population densities. This philosophy would continue to be influential in the post-war New Town Movement of which Newton Aycliffe became Lord Beveridge's favoured example.

In 1940 Ernest Bevin asked Beveridge to take over the Welfare Department in his Ministry of Labour. In 1942 Beveridge and his staff produced the so-called Beveridge Report – its official title was Social Insurance and Allied Services. This report identified the five 'Giant Evils' in society - squalor, ignorance, want, idleness, and disease. The report came during the middle of the Second World War and promised multiple social reforms to reward those serving in the military for their sacrifice.

It formed the basis of the post-war Welfare State which included: the Family Allowances Act 1945, the National Insurance (Industrial Injuries) Act 1946, the National Insurance Act 1946, the National Health Service Act 1946, the Pensions (Increase) Act 1947, the Landlord and Tenant (Rent Control) Act 1949, the National Insurance (Industrial Injuries) Act 1948, and the National Insurance Act 1949. Prior to the end of the war the Churchill government recognised the need to resolve the impending housing crisis. Three million homes were destroyed during the war and would require rapid replacement. Prefabricated homes and non-conventional, concrete block construction methods would help resolve this problem – in the short term.

The end of the Second World War again precipitated significant change in the Great Aycliffe area. The munitions factory at ROF 59 stopped producing munitions and needed repurposing (it was taken over by North Eastern Trading Estates Limited), a large number of military personnel returned and needed jobs, the Labour Party headed by Clement Atlee came into power and chose to implement the suggestions of the Beveridge Report.

On the 1st August 1946 the Government approved the New Towns Act that was designed to facilitate the creation of new towns as part of the relocation of people from devastated city centres – nine of these new towns were around London.

The three key components of the New Towns Act were a new form of agency backed by central government, compulsory powers to buy the required land and access to 'patient money' (money which could wait for a return as initial development drove budgets into deficit). Newton Aycliffe and Peterlee in County Durham and East Kilbride in Scotland were the only initial designations outside of the circum – London area. Newton Aycliffe was envisaged as a new town to house a labour force for the evolving former munitions works as it changed to a light industrial complex. Each new town was placed under the governance of its own Development Corporation with the expectation that control would shift to an elected Town Council after the build was complete. The Development Corporations had powers of compulsory purchase to acquire the required land as well as the budget for house construction.

The initial Aycliffe Development Corporation was established on the 2nd July 1947 and consisted of Lord Beveridge (Chairman), W.N. Davis (Vice Chairman), A.J. Alsopp, T.J. Cahill, T. Benfold and G.C. Summerson. Initial site selection for the housing of Newton Aycliffe was not without difficulties (Boyes, 2007). Two sites were initially considered one north of the Clarence Railway and then a second to the south of the trading estate nearer to Aycliffe Village.

Both sites were generally flat and were poor quality farmland. The southern site had the advantage of only being under the jurisdiction of Darlington Rural District Council. However mineral rights complicated land ownership of the southern site associated with magnesian limestone quarrying as well as the potential for noise and dust pollution. The northern site was at the nexus of three councils: Darlington RDC, Sedgefield RDC and Shildon UDC making for more complex administrative negotiations. In addition the northern site had a high-tension power line crossing it, which would require removing. Despite this Lord Beveridge insisted on the northern site. This decision was partly driven by a desire for the new town to never be perceived as a suburb of Darlington or a so-called 'ribbon development' along the Great North Road to Darlington. The initial area was 867 acres in a triangle bounded by Woodham Burn (in the northwest), The Great North Road (to the east) and The Clarence Railway (in the south).

The former munitions factories quickly began to house new businesses. By August 1946 some 60 firms had set up in business and employed many people – all of whom travelled to the industrial estate from housing in more removed towns and villages. The Grenfell – Baines report (1949) contains an analysis of where workers travelled from for jobs on the new trading estate.

Figure 28 - One of few pictures of the countryside on the future site of Newton Aycliffe prior to its construction. The view is the bridge carrying New Lane over Woodham Burn in summer 1948. Today this location would be on Stephenson Way taken from near Stephenson Way Primary School looking NW. (Photo from the Grenfell Baines Report)

The catchment area was throughout the mining areas of east and west Durham as well as a significant number from Darlington. Businesses were attracted by relatively low rents and the availability of sites ranging from small to large. This continued to emphasise the need for local housing. Early factories were Bakclite, Chemical Compounds, Banda, and Toledo-Woodhead Springs. Appendix 3 provides a list of businesses operating on the Trading Estate in 1951 and indicates that something close to 3000 people were employed there at that time. Bakelite opened in 1948 and began making plastics which was a relatively new substance and dangerous to make. Significant alterations to existing war era buildings were required but some of the original buildings still exist on the trading estate.

On the 12th February 1947 it was publicly announced that the government had the intention of building a new town at Aycliffe. The Aycliffe New Town Designation Order was made on 19th April 1947 and Newton Aycliffe became the fifth of six new towns designated before the end of 1947 (the others in order of designation were Stevenage, Crawley, Hemel Hempstead, Harlow and East Kilbride).

The Grenfell – Baines Group was contracted to develop the first Master Plan for the New Town. On the 21st March 1949 they submitted the plan to the Rt. Hon. Lewis Silkin the then minster of Town and Country Planning. The original design was described in The Newtonian Volume 1, No. 2 in an editorial by Reverend Tom Drewette. The design was based on fixing three problems of urban life to that point. i) Retain an element of country living, ii) avoid social segregation (of the type that produced rich 'west ends' and poor 'east ends' and iii) Increase the leisure of housewives by designing labour saving houses and arranging better facilities for shopping, washing and child care.

The Master Plan divided the town into five wards (A, B, C, D and E) with a general section providing services for all town residents. Each Ward was to contain about 650 dwellings of all types (flats, old peoples homes, houses etc.) to accommodate about 2600 people. This projected a total population of 13,000 that exceeded the original plan by 3000. The Wards were further divided into precincts with about six precincts per Ward and therefore 110 dwellings and 450 people. Each precinct was designed to have open green spaces and limited through roads. The Master Plan was subsequently modified in 1957 and again in 1963 with proposed population increases both times.

A slightly bizarre aspect of social engineering was undertaken in the planning for Newton Aycliffe when a consultant (Professor Dennis Chapman) was asked to determine the best way of having people of diverse socio-economic backgrounds live together in the Wards (Boyes, 2007). The idea was to have managers (assumed to be more well-off) living next to labourers (assumed to be less well-off). Ultimately the residents of the town moved around and established a 'natural order' for themselves – generally moving next to and amongst people of similar backgrounds.

Philipson (1988) provides a more detailed discussion of the formative years and ongoing political intrigue as Newton Aycliffe was conceived and developed.

Chapter Five

The Pioneer Years (1948 – 1963)

As described earlier the post-war New Towns were an extension of the Garden City movement of the early 20th century. They themselves were an extension of towns built by philanthropist industrialists to house workers for their factories in the 18th and 19th centuries (Cadbury, Lever etc.). The basic design model was to create a series of village-like settings with low density housing around a village green with easy access to basic shops and amenities. Lord Beveridge also pressed the case for making the life of the 'housewife' significantly easier. Initially his plans called for communal washing and laundry facilities but a survey of housewives indicated that they preferred to do laundry in their own homes. The plan was modified to make washers available on a rental basis to each resident. Once planning approvals were obtained and construction commenced things moved reasonably quickly despite post-war restrictions on building supplies and limitations on the availability of skilled building workers.

Parallel to the construction of housing for workers was the ongoing growth of the Industrial Estate and the jobs it created. On the 20th July 1948 Harold Wilson (then a junior minister but to become Prime Minister) opened one of Newton Aycliffe's major factories – Bakelite. The availability of labour was also initially an issue with competing industrial estates and chemical plants (at Teesside and Wilton) attracting the unemployed in those areas. The collapse of coal mining in southwest Durham provided an increased flux of workers into the 1960s – the final mines of substance in the area were closed by 1968.

Throughout this time the amount of rent being paid in Newton Aycliffe was a contentious issue for its residents. Initially they were going to be similar to those in adjacent communities but a series of rises were needed to account for the capital expenditure on new houses in Newton Aycliffe. The Development Corporation always tried to rationalise the increases as the cost to live in superior quality homes and by 1957 the tenants seemed to have accepted this thesis and their complaints waned.

The remainder of this chapter will be discussed on a year-by-year basis because so much rapid change was achieved each year. The information for this section is material largely derived from early editions of the town newssheet 'The Newtonian' as well as progress speeches by the Community Association and the Development Corporation.

Lord Beveridge as Chairman of the first Aycliffe Development Corporation received copies of most of the paperwork generated in the early years of Newton Aycliffe. His archive is retained in the library of The London School of Economics and has provided most of the information cited in this section. In addition the New Town published handbooks for tenants in alternate years from 1953, 1955, 1957, 1959, 1961 and later from which data has also been used.

A series of aerial photographs were taken during the years of Newton Aycliffe's growth. In the Durham County Record Office are a series of these photographs and some have precise dates. There were photographic over flights on the following dates: 17th May 1951, 4th June 1952, 18th September 1953, September 1954, 14th September 1955, April 1957, 22nd May 1958, May 1959, unspecified date 1962, 2 – 3rd April 1964, unspecified date 1973, 20th October 1975, 6 – 16th July 1977 and 29th April 1980. These aerial photos can be used to date certain construction events based on presence or absence of structures whose construction date is known.

Pioneer residents of Newton Aycliffe had little to work with when it came to public buildings. The Gretna Green Wedding Inn on the Great North Road provided a place to socialise and a wooden Methodist Chapel at Simpasture (approximately where the shops stand today) was the only other public building. The Blacksmiths Arms near Preston-Le-Skerne (known locally as the 'Hammer and Pincers') was also a popular summer destination for a Sunday walk. The Clarence Farm complex (Farmhouse, adjoining cottages and a barn) became the core of early social gathering. Two shops were opened on one end of the barns and the remainder was converted into a Community Centre. In addition a number of mobile facilities provided services to early residents: coal deliveries, grocery vans (Broughs, Co-op), milk delivery, library van.

The farmhouse itself became the first Church of England (St. Clare's) and upstairs rooms were used as meeting rooms.

Aerial view of the Clarence Farm Complex that was at the heart of social life in early Newton Aycliffe - picture probably dates at 17th May 1951 with the local area all under construction. (Photo from Great Aycliffe Town Council)

The creation of something from nothing, particularly an entire new town requires leadership and hard work. In the case of Newton Aycliffe this was provided in the earliest years by a number of important individuals. These are the type of people who embrace the concept and volunteer to help at every turn despite having permanent day jobs. They were 'the glue' that kept the concept of Newton Aycliffe together during its earliest and hardest days. The following individuals have impressed this author as having been critical to the development of Newton Aycliffe:

Lord William Henry Beveridge – The man with the 'social vision' to create the concept of Newton Aycliffe. Born on March 5th 1879 and he taught at L.S.E. in the 1930s entering government during the Second World War. He designed the post-war social system that controls many aspects of UK life to this day. He and his wife lived on the town for a couple of years at 5, Bede Crescent and they participated in many openings, tree plantings, dedications and social events on the early town. They moved back to Oxford and Edinburgh in 1953. Lord Beveridge passed away on March 16th 1963 at the age of 84.

Joseph Leslie Moore – Secretary of Aycliffe Development Corporation. The 'mover and shaker' who dealt with many of the day-to-day issues that arose in the new town. There are many letters from Mr. Moore to Lord Beveridge discussing things as diverse as shipping goods back to the Beveridge's after they left the town, the sale of Beveridge's land next to Woodham Burn and the possibility of joining 5 and 6 Bede Crescent into a single house for the Beveridge's.

Frank Hiley – Chief Finance Officer of Aycliffe Development Corporation. An ambitious and highly skilled financial officer. He applied for a number of jobs around the country during his tenure at Aycliffe Development Corporation and always got glowing references from Lord Beveridge. The Hiley family lived at 33, Gilpin Road and Frank passed away in late 1978.

Miss E.M.B. Hamilton – Housing Section of Aycliffe Development Corporation. She was an Oxford graduate and had a certificate from the Royal Institute of Chartered Surveyors. She provided the quality control to the new town. She routinely inspected gardens and provided feedback when things were not up to scratch. She also organised and executed the Welcome Parties that introduced new tenants to their fellow pioneers as well as the many clubs and organisations on the town. At some point she lived in the corner of Clarence Green. In later life she moved to Killingworth Village. In the 29th November 1974 issue of the 'The Newton News/Newtonian' she provided a photograph of Lord Beveridge's headstone in Thockrington, Northumberland.

Andrew Morton – Chief Horticultural Officer of Aycliffe Development Corporation. Provided design and implementation for all the green spaces around Newton Aycliffe. Lived at No 1, Clarence Corner.

Figure 30 - Reverend Thomas Anderson Drewette 1912 – 1961 (Photo from St. Clare's 25th anniversary brochure)

Donald Vickers – Chairman of Great Aycliffe Parish Council, Chairman of Newton Aycliffe Community Association. Presented an annual overview of community activities for a number of years. Don began his working life as a coal miner at age 14 and returned to that after the war. However he did external courses at Durham University and eventually became a Justice of the Peace in 1955. He was also on the board of governors of Aycliffe Approved School. Lived at 22, Clarence Chare.

Harry Bilton – Council administrator and Secretary of the Gardens Guild. To many in the oldest part of Newton Aycliffe Harry was the liaison to 'all things council'. He was willing and able to help many people and was well liked by all. Lived at 4, Clarence Green and then 3, Clarence Close. A personal memory: In the mid 1960s Harry's son Geoff and I did a walking tour of Snowdonia. Harry personally booked all the youth hostels, meals and trains to make this possible. At that time it was all done by letter – no online booking or emails! As the Aycliffe Development Corporation was closed down Harry preserved many artefacts from the history of the New Town that would have otherwise ended up discarded. He retired in mid 1978 after 30 years of service.

Reverend Thomas Anderson Drewette – First Church of England vicar of St. Clare's Church and first editor of 'The Newtonian'. Initially lived at 1, Clarence Chare and then moved into the new vicarage at St. Clare's. An ever-present at all early events in the town and he edited 'The Newtonian' with the explicit goal of documenting the early history of Newton Aycliffe as well as keeping residents informed of events. A very familiar figure on the new town he was often called 'the man in black'. He sadly passed away on the 6th April 1961 at the relatively young age of 49.

1948
The Beginning

Cutting the first sod -
28th June, 1948.

Figure 31 - The official 'sod cutting' ceremony, 28th June 1948. The vice chairman of the Aycliffe Development Corporation, W.N. Davis is wielding the spade. Harry Bilton is third from the right. Several photos were taken of this event and poses change slightly. (Photo courtesy of Great Aycliffe Town Council)

In March 1948, Lord Beveridge became the first Chairman of Aycliffe Development Corporation. This appointment has been cited (Boyes, 2007) as a significant reason why local councils were less hostile to the building of Newton Aycliffe than councils associated with other new towns. Beveridge's reputation from his work during the Second World War meant he was well liked by politicians of all parties. Additional Aycliffe Development Corporation members were: William Neil Davis (former headmaster of St. Helen's Auckland school, previously chairman of Bishop Auckland Urban District Council), Mrs. T.J. Cahill (a Fellow of the Royal Institute of British Architects and partner in the firm of Reavell and Cahill, architects of Alnwick and Newcastle upon Tyne), A.J. Alsop (partner in the firm of Alsop and Eltringham, accountants of Darlington and alderman of Darlington Borough Council), T. Benfold (a justice of the peace from Ferryhill), G.C. Gibson (from Shildon) and G.C. Summerson (another justice of the peace and managing director of Summerson and sons Ltd). He was also a member of and previous chairman of Darlington Rural District Council.

In 1948 there was a brief plan to provide centrally generated universal heating for the homes to be built in Newton Aycliffe (Boyes, 2007). This would have used the old boiler house from R.O.F. 59 (shown in Figure 16) and a network of pipework to connect the houses. The plan was abandoned by 1949 when the price of the boiler house proved too high and local councils complained that it might reduce sales of coal on the town.

The sod-cutting ceremony was held on the 28th June 1948. Rather famously the commemorative spade and turf box went missing in 1995/1996 and were only returned in 2009 after being fortuitously 'found' in the attic of a former Town Clerk (see page 129).

The precise location of this ceremony has not been documented but looking at the event photos it seems likely that it was at Clarence Green – the large trees look like those on Clarence Chare, the hedging would have been along New Lane and the farm house in the background could be Field House. The passage of time has also made it difficult to connect the names of participants on the spade with the faces in the photographs.

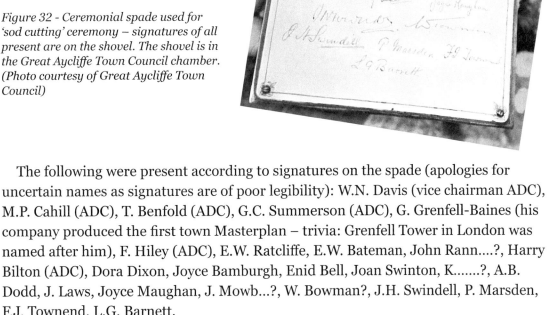

Figure 32 - Ceremonial spade used for 'sod cutting' ceremony – signatures of all present are on the shovel. The shovel is in the Great Aycliffe Town Council chamber. (Photo courtesy of Great Aycliffe Town Council)

The following were present according to signatures on the spade (apologies for uncertain names as signatures are of poor legibility): W.N. Davis (vice chairman ADC), M.P. Cahill (ADC), T. Benfold (ADC), G.C. Summerson (ADC), G. Grenfell-Baines (his company produced the first town Masterplan – trivia: Grenfell Tower in London was named after him), F. Hiley (ADC), E.W. Ratcliffe, E.W. Bateman, John Rann....?, Harry Bilton (ADC), Dora Dixon, Joyce Bamburgh, Enid Bell, Joan Swinton, K.......?, A.B. Dodd, J. Laws, Joyce Maughan, J. Mowb...?, W. Bowman?, J.H. Swindell, P. Marsden, F.J. Townend, L.G. Barnett.

The first houses that were quickly built in Newton Aycliffe were 41 prefabricated, aluminium-framed bungalows (Prefabs) built around the first two greens at Clarence Green and Travellers' Green. Lillian Holmes (as interviewed by Edwards, 1968) can recall these pre-fabs being delivered on lorries and placed on site. These Prefabs were part of a general strategy for rapidly implementing new housing stock. The type selected were so-called AIROH Prefabs, built of aluminium, about 675 square feet in area and containing hot and cold water with a bathroom and kitchen as part of a utility module. They even had a fridge that was something only two percent of UK houses had at the time. They were built in a former aircraft assembly plant and could be installed on-site in four to eight hours! The number were probably limited to 41 because by that time the unit cost was about £1610 and thought to be expensive relative to other available construction methods. Each Prefab also had a shed associated with it. The original Prefabs had a soft metal cladding that was coloured either pink or light blue. Since there were no main drains and sewers in the New Town in 1948 / 1949 the Prefabs were temporarily connected to a cesspool. An example of this type of Prefab has been preserved at the St. Fagan's National Museum of History near Cardiff, Wales.

AYCLIFFE DEVELOPMENT CORPORATION

MEMBERS:
Rt. Hon. Lord Beveridge, K.C.B., F.B.A.
(Chairman)
W. N. Davis, O.B.E. (Vice-Chairman)
Mrs. T. J. Cahill, F.R.I.B.A.
A. J. Alsop, F.C.R.A., F.C.I.S.
T. Benfold, C.B.E., J.P.
G. C. Gibson.
T. H. Summerson, J. P.

Reply should be addressed:
For the attention of the ....

ASTANCE
NEWR...
N. DA...
Co. D....AM.

Telephone: Aycliffe 3261.

2nd November, 1948.

Dear Mr. and Mrs. Charlesworth,

As Chairman of the Aycliffe Development Corporation and on behalf of the Members of the Corporation, it is my privilege to welcome you as one of the first citizens of Newton Aycliffe.

Many of you will be aware from press reports, of the aim of the Corporation in building the new town. Briefly, we hope to make a town in which the advantages of town and country life will be combined, with houses of modern design incorporating the most up-to-date labour-saving devices, each with its own garden and grouped round village greens, with easy access to work, with convenient centres for shopping and entertainment and study, and meeting one's neighbours.

But this cannot come at once. You all know the difficulties of shortages of all kinds with which we in Britain are having to struggle. Nor whatever we of the Corporation do, can we make Newton Aycliffe as we want to make it - one of the happiest towns in Durham, without the active help of the people who live there. A town is made by its inhabitants, not by its bricks and mortar or its aluminium.

We hope that you, who come in as its first inhabitants, in the pre-fabricated houses that we have been able to provide as a first step, will regard yourselves as pioneers of a new movement, and will have time to be interested, not merely in making your own homes as pleasant as they can be made, but in helping to make the whole town, as it grows, a happy and beautiful town.

Contd.

In the near future, a model of the Corporation's proposals will be exhibited, and your comments and criticisms will be invited. Please remember this is YOUR town and the Corporation earnestly desires your co-operation in helping to make Newton Aycliffe "the shining star of the North", and a model for all other new towns in the Country.

In conclusion may I offer my personal good wishes to you and express the hope that your stay here will be long, happy and prosperous.

Yours sincerely,

Beveridge

Chairman.

Mr. and Mrs. W. Charlesworth,
c/o Toledo Woodhead Springs Ltd.,
Aycliffe Trading Estate,
Nr. Darlington.

Figure 33 - Actual letter from Lord Beveridge congratulating early resident 'pioneers' Bill and Joyce Charlesworth on the award of tenancy of 10, Clarence Green on 2nd November 1948. (Photo courtesy David Charlesworth)

54

At 11:30am on Tuesday the 9th November 1948, an official opening ceremony and service of dedication was held at the first Prefab supposedly to be occupied (by Mr. and Mrs. Don G. Perry – an ex army captain). The ceremony was held at No. 20, Clarence Green, however the Perrys eventually occupied No. 9 since there was room for a garage there! When interviewed by The Northern Echo in 1998 on the occasion of their Golden Wedding Anniversary, the Perrys described the great mix of people on Clarence Green in those early years, 'There was an architect, a miner and people who worked on the Trading Estate – it was all very friendly. I remember because we were the only people who had a car, a friend and myself used to go to everyone in the street and ask if they wanted fish and chips. The nearest fish and chip shop was in Chilton.' The Dorman family subsequently moved into No. 20; Nos. 20, 22 and 23 Clarence Green were open for inspection on the opening day. Lord Beveridge gave a speech and also planted an oak tree on Clarence Green (location now unknown!). Figure 34 shows the program of events from the dedication ceremony.

The first 41 families that inhabited these prefabricated, small homes 'in a sea of mud' must be regarded as 'True Pioneers' since when they moved into Newton Aycliffe it had no facilities whatsoever and barely existed as a concept. Through the 1950s new residents were also pioneering but with an ever increasing infrastructure.

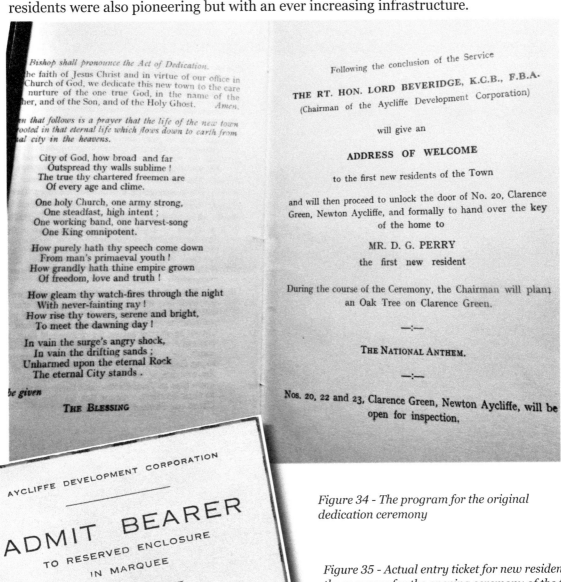

Figure 34 - The program for the original dedication ceremony

Figure 35 - Actual entry ticket for new residents to the marquee for the opening ceremony of the first bungalow (photo courtesy of David Charlesworth).

Figure 36 - Dedication of the first prefab at 11:30am on Tuesday the 9th November 1948. (Photo from Aycliffe Village Local History website with permission).

Figure 37 - Typical Aluminium Prefabricated bungalow (Prefab) of the first generation – the example shown is 15, Clarence Green with proud occupant Eva Creaney at the door.

Figure 36 shows the actual opening ceremony with the Bishop of Jarrow on the left and Lord Beveridge in the doorway of No. 20 Clarence Green. Don Perry is in the wheelchair.

Jim and Eva Creaney provide a typical case study of the early pioneers in Newton Aycliffe (and one I actually know something about!). Both were in the Royal Navy as the Second World War ended and they met as they were being demobbed in Sheerness, Kent. Jim was from the east end of Glasgow and Eva was from a typical mining family in Crook, Co Durham. They got engaged and were married in Crook on the 6th December 1947 and 'lived in' with Eva's parents. Jim was offered work at Roddymoor mine but not having been brought up in a mining tradition, he declined and took work digging ditches in Weardale. He then got a job at the Iron Foundry on Aycliffe Trading Estate and according to the newly developed points system (described on page 73) he and Eva qualified for and took possession of a Prefab at 15, Clarence Green in late 1948. (Figure 37)

The garden associated with the Prefab proved troublesome for Jim, who'd never gardened before, and the infamous Miss Hamilton insisted on tidy gardens! In the summer of 1953, they moved across the green into 20, Clarence Chare where they remained until Jim passed away in 1995. Eva continued to live there until she moved to a bungalow in Pease Way before her death in 2012.

Most of the original occupants of the Prefabs will have similar stories to that of the Creaneys.

The maps shown in Figures 38 and 39 are of unknown origin (they were found in Mrs. Eva Creaney's possessions upon her death in 2012). They are dated 19th October 1949 and document the original occupants of the 41 Prefabs around Clarence and Travellers' Greens. Clearly they have been used to monitor where people moved to when they left the Prefabs. They also show the anticipated numbering of surrounding housing.

Very early in Newton Aycliffe's history a decision was made that no roads would be called 'streets' – there are roads, chares, a parade, a gate, closes, walks, crescents, greens but no streets. I haven't come across any documentation of this being a conscious decision but it has become a Newton Aycliffe 'thing'. As the town began to evolve a series of metal plaques were made describing where the road names came from. These were mounted in small seating areas, one being near the garages at Bede Crescent (named after the Venerable Bede of course) – they have now been moved and are on the wall inside the Oakleaf Centre.

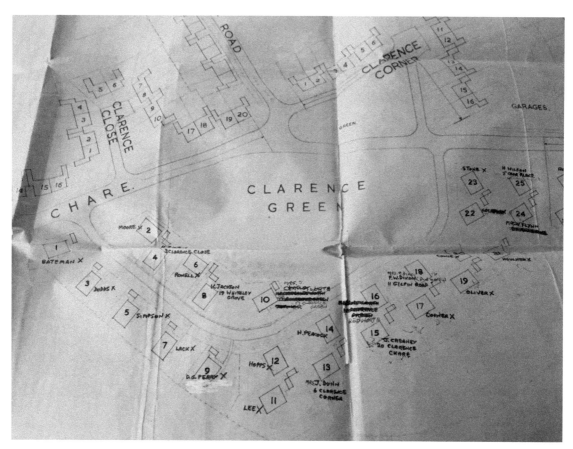

Figure 38 - An original plan of Clarence Green identifying locations and addresses of each Prefab as well as names of occupants in October 1949. Later edits describe where these original occupants relocated.

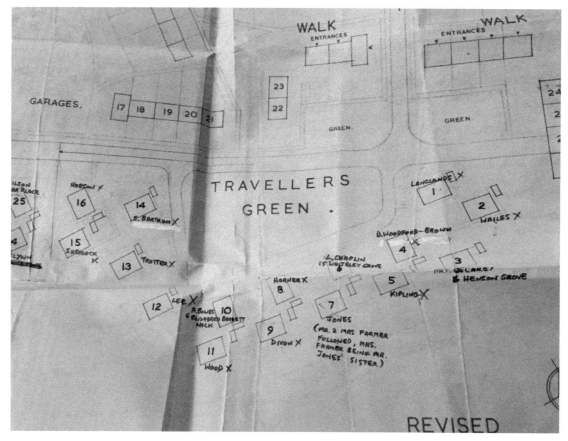

Figure 39 - An original plan of Travellers' Green identifying locations and addresses of each Prefab as well as names of occupants in October 1949. Later edits describe where these original occupants relocated.

Figure 40 - View to the west along Clarence Green. The house immediately to the left of the tree is the gable end of No. 10 Clarence Green, originally occupied by the Charlesworth family.

Conditions of Tenancy

1.—The tenancy shall be a weekly one in all cases ending 12 o'clock noon on any Saturday and without prejudice to Clause 17, determinable by one week's notice in writing by either the Corporation or the Tenant, such notice to be given by or to the GENERAL MANAGER before 12 o'clock noon on any Saturday.

2. The rents are due and payable in advance on Saturday in each week. The Collector will collect the rents weekly and give receipts therefor on a rent card. Receipts for rents will only be recognised which are given on the special rent cards to be supplied to the Tenant for the purpose. The Tenant must produce the rent card whenever required so to do.

3.—The tenancy shall, where appropriate, be a joint one in the names of the householder and his wife.

4.—Without the permission of the Corporation, the Tenant shall not use the premises other than as a private dwelling house and garden, or exhibit any business notice, sign or advertisement. The front gardens or forecourt shall not be used as a drying ground.

5.—The Tenant will not be permitted to underlet, assign or part with the possession of the premises or any part thereof without the permission of the Corporation.

6.—The Tenant shall be responsible for keeping in proper condition (damage by reasonable wear and tear and fire excepted) the boundary fences, hedges, paving, glass windows, gas and electricity fittings and other fittings and shall leave the same in good repair and condition on quitting, and shall before quitting have the house properly cleaned to the satisfaction of the Corporation and if the Tenant make default the Corporation may execute such repairs and cleansing as aforesaid and charge the cost thereof to the Tenant.

7.—Any part of the premises, including fences, paving, fittings and fixtures damaged by the Tenant or through his negligence, or by the installation or removal of furniture and other effects, will be repaired by the Corporation at the cost of the Tenant.

8.—No wireless aerial shall be erected without the permission of the Corporation and only on such conditions as the Corporation may determine.

9.—The Tenant shall take every precaution for the prevention of damage by fire or by the bursting of water pipes.

10.—The Tenant shall be responsible for the interior decorations during the tenancy.

11.—The Tenant shall not make any addition to, or structural alterations in the house or premises, or erect any toolhouse, shed, greenhouse, fowlhouse, pigeon cote or other building (except a garden cold frame not more than three feet high) within the garden, without the consent of the Corporation.

12.—The Tenant shall give immediate notice to the Corporation of any stoppage in the drains. The placing in the W.C. of rags, cotton, bottles or anything likely to choke it or the drain, is strictly prohibited. In the case of violation of this condition the expense of cleaning the W.C. or drain will be charged to the Tenant.

13.—Ashes and dry refuse only are to be thrown into the dust bins. All vegetable refuse must be burned, or retained under cover for collection as salvage.

14.—The Tenant shall keep the front and back gardens cultivated and in a clean and orderly condition, and all grass, trees, shrubs and hedges shall be cut, trimmed or pruned at the proper season and when necessary. Open forecourts, where provided, will be maintained by the Corporation but the Tenant will be expected to assist in their preservation by preventing damage to them.

15.—The Tenant shall not cut down or remove any trees or shrubs once planted on the premises without the consent of the Corporation.

16.—No pigeons, doves, poultry, pigs or any animals (except cats and dogs) shall be kept on the premises without the consent of the Corporation. Owners of cats and dogs shall keep their animals under proper control and shall not allow them to be a nuisance to other residents of the town or to cause damage to public greens, forecourts, etc.

17.—If any weekly payment of rent shall be in arrear for more than seven days, it shall be lawful for the Corporation to re-enter on the premises and forthwith determine the tenancy without giving any notice to quit.

18.—The Tenant shall be responsible for all present and future Rates and Taxes ordinarily payable by the Tenant.

19.—The Corporation shall be at liberty by their agents or workmen upon due notice being given, and on production of a proper authority, to enter and inspect the state of repair and cleanliness of any house at all reasonable hours of the day and execute any repairs therein.

20.—Any Tenant, who in the opinion of the Corporation, shall neglect to observe these conditions or misuse, overcrowd, or improperly occupy any house or causes or creates any discomfort or inconvenience to the neighbours, shall be subject to notice under Clause 1 without a remedy of any kind on account of such notice, and the Corporation shall not be liable for any claim by such Tenant for any damage arising therefrom.

21.—The entry into possession by a Tenant shall be conclusive evidence as against such Tenant of his concurrence in and acceptance of all the foregoing conditions and of his agreement to be bound thereby.

22.—As these conditions are made for the mutual benefit of all tenants of houses in the town they are particularly requested to see that they are conformed to in all respects and the amenities of the Town preserved.

IMPORTANT.—It is most important that this Card be produced when a payment is made, but if for any reason it is not available, the Collector will issue a Temporary Official Receipt, to be afterwards exchanged for the usual entry on the Card.

AYCLIFFE DEVELOPMENT CORPORATION

1948-49

Tenant's Rent Card   Ref. No.............

Tenant's Name William and Joyce CHARLESWORTH.

Address 10, Clarence Green, Newton Aycliffe.

Commencement of Tenancy 13-11-48

Net Rent	17s. 0d.	per week
Rates	2s. 4d.	,,
Water	8d.	,,
TOTAL RENT ... Referred to as "Rent" within this Rent Card	£1.0s. 0d.	,,

1. Name and Address of the Medical Officer of Health :—

   Dr. Wm. RODGERS, 53, Coniscliffe Road, Darlington

2. Name and Address of the Landlord :—

   AYCLIFFE DEVELOPMENT CORPORATION

   Simpasture, Aycliffe

Summary of Secs. 58, 59 & 61 of the Housing Act, 1936

1. An occupier who causes or permits his dwelling to be overcrowded is liable to prosecution for an offence under the Housing Act, 1936, and, if convicted, to a fine not exceeding five pounds. Any part of a house which is occupied by a separate family is a "dwelling."

2. A dwelling is overcrowded if the number of persons sleeping in it is more than the "permitted number," or is such that two or more of those persons, being ten years old or over, of opposite sexes (not being persons living together as husband and wife), must sleep in the same room.

3. The "permitted number" for the dwelling to which this Payment Card relates is............ 5 persons. In counting the number of persons each child under ten years of age counts as half a person, and a child of less than one year is not counted at all.

4. The Act contains special provisions relating to overcrowding already existing or which is due to a child attaining the age of either one or ten years, or which is due to exceptional circumstances. Full information about these special provisions and all provisions as to overcrowding can be obtained free on application to the Local Authority whose address is printed on this card.

473746   ALFRED GILBERT & SONS, LTD., LONDON, N.W.9

Figure 41 - Actual Rent Book from No. 10 Clarence Green in 1948. Notice the long list of tenancy conditions. (Photo courtesy of David Charlesworth.)

1949

Figure 42 - A photo across New Lane / Clarence Chare to the newly built Prefabs – the photo was likely taken in 1949 during the laying of main drainage sewers. (Photo courtesy of Great Aycliffe Town Council).

Figure 43 - View from the Prefabs across Clarence Green to the construction of two story ORLIT/UNITY houses in Clarence Corner (Photo taken in 1949 and courtesy Great Aycliffe Town Council) – Clarence Corner houses are still in scaffolding. It seems that Clarence Chare has not been started.

60

Physical Growth

According to the Reverend Tom Drewette in his editorial in 'The Newtonian', Volume 1, number 2, these Prefabs remained the only houses (in addition to two houses in Clarence Corner) that were occupied until the end of 1949. This was confirmed by the Darlington Rural District Annual Report for 1949. These residents were therefore the first 'true' pioneers who moved in to a totally undeveloped town. In a speech given by Lord Beveridge in 1951 he summarised 1949 as a year when main drains and sewerage pipes were being laid in preparation for subsequent building. Apparently the main drains and sewers had cost £120,000. He also cited materials and supply shortages and weather and site conditions as slowing building progress, particularly steel shortages related to rearmament needs. Darlington Rural District Council (1949) also cited a lack of qualified tradesmen as another impediment to progress and suggested that new housing should be prioritised for such workers.

The post-Prefab construction began in Clarence Corner, Clarence Chare and Clarence Close and these houses were also a non-conventional type. They were two story, so-called ORLIT or UNITY construction – meaning a series of evenly spaced reinforced concrete pillars with 'blown' breeze block type units inserted between them to form walls. The windows and doors were made to fit the uniform spacing of the pillars that also acted as mullions and door-frames. Roofs were of normal wood and tile construction. This type of house was built sporadically across much of the older part of the town. Many years later some of these houses were found to be 'corroding' (reinforcing steel was rusting, expanding and cracking the concrete) and becoming structurally unsafe. Many were demolished and new houses rebuilt in their place (see figure 44). The earliest models in Clarence Chare, Clarence Close, Clarence Corner and Baliol Road were ultimately found to be structurally sound and are there today.

According to 'The Newtonian' (Vol. 1, No. 6) by the end of 1949 the only new houses occupied in the town were the 41 Prefabs in Clarence and Travellers' Greens plus two houses in Clarence Corner and these housed a total of 125 people. There were also the 21 older farms and cottages whose population was approximately 85. Thus the total population of Newton Aycliffe was about 210.

Figure 44 - A Later generation of ORLIT/UNITY Houses built on Shafto Way (on the right of the photo) near Neville Parade shopping Centre – These were found to be structurally defective and were demolished and replaced in the 1980s. (Reproduced by permission of Durham County Record Office D/CL 5/1672)

The only public buildings in the town were the old wooden Methodist Chapel at Simpasture and the Gretna Green Wedding Inn on the Great North Road.

As building began to ramp-up, a pleasant by-product was the accumulation of 'mounds' of removed topsoil etc. This created the only topography in the New Town which children happily used for tobogganing, cycling etc. Examples were at Lee Green, behind the flats on Baliol Green (the so-called 'Seven Hills') and between Clarence Green and the railway.

Possibly the first report of local pollution was reported in the Darlington Rural District Annual Report for 1949 where a spillage of paint and distemper into Demon's Beck was reported. This would become an ongoing problem as the Trading Estate developed.

Social Development

The citizens of Newton Aycliffe quickly recognised the need for an organisation that would represent their interests to the Aycliffe Development Corporation. On January 17th 1949 the newly formed Clarence Farm Pioneer Community Association of Newton Aycliffe held its first meeting at the Gretna Green Wedding Inn. This was where they held their bigger meetings for some time with their smaller meetings being in members' homes. It was only when the Clarence Farm Complex became operational as a Community Centre in September 1950 that meetings stopped being held in the Gretna.

The first children born in Newton Aycliffe arrived in the first quarter of 1949. Carolyn Corner and Alan Dixon were both born in the quarter, with Carolyn being the first to be born on the town, whereas Alan was born at his grandma's house off the town, although his parents lived in a Prefab at the time. Alan went on to live his entire life on the town and died in 2014 at the age of 66.

The first anniversary birthday party was held at the Gretna to celebrate the founding of Newton Aycliffe.

Figure 45 - An original invitation to the first birthday party of Newton Aycliffe (photo courtesy of David Charlesworth)

Figure 46 - An early photograph of the Gretna Green Wedding Inn, the very earliest centre of social life in the Pioneer's Newton Aycliffe. (Photo courtesy of Great Aycliffe Town Council, circa early 1950s)

Figure 47 - An evening out at the Gretna – From left to right Harry Bilton, Ernie Tennick, Eva Creaney, Doreen Tennick and Jim Creaney. Probably early 1950s.

1950

Physical Growth

This year was to prove a time of rapid growth once the sewage and drainage systems were in place.

According to a summary of 1950 progress in 'The Newtonian' (Vol. 1, No. 6 – February, 1951) by the end of March 1950 the occupation of Clarence Corner was complete and the occupation of Clarence Chare and Baliol Road had begun. By May the first residents moved into Hackworth Close and the Reverend Drewette took up residence in No. 1 Clarence Chare. In June Baliol Green began to be occupied. Towards the end of July the first residents began to occupy Anne Swyft Road. In September the first house in Westcott Walk was occupied. Early in November, Elizabeth Barrett Walk and Havelock Close began to be occupied and then just before the end of the year, two houses in Surtees Walk were occupied. All this building activity brought the total number of houses occupied by the end of 1950 to 139, with a population of 439. There still remained the older farms and cottages and adding them into the total brought the number of houses to 160 with about 524 people.

Figure 48 - Aerial photo circa 1950 / 1951 showing the earliest construction in the older part of Newton Aycliffe. The Clarence Farm Complex is in the upper left; the road that will become St. Cuthbert's Way does not yet go under the Railway. (Photo courtesy Great Aycliffe Town Council).

In 1950 a significant effort was put in by the Aycliffe Development Corporation to scope out the possibility of establishing hostels for single workers. An architect designed a 200 room fully serviced apartment complex. Sadly, the single workers on the trading estate showed little interest and the scheme was abandoned. The Aycliffe Development Corporation decided to lodge single men in a number of five-bedroomed houses as boarding houses and they proposed to build blocks of 8 – 10 bed-sitting rooms for single females.

Figure 49 - A Portrait of the Reverend Thomas Anderson Drewette from 1955 – photo from Chapman, 1995

Figure 50 - Clarence Farm – this became derelict as the New Town encroached on it. Its rooms became used as meeting rooms, the Church of St. Clare and a reading room in the evolving Clarence Farm Community Centre. (Photo from Chapman, 1995)

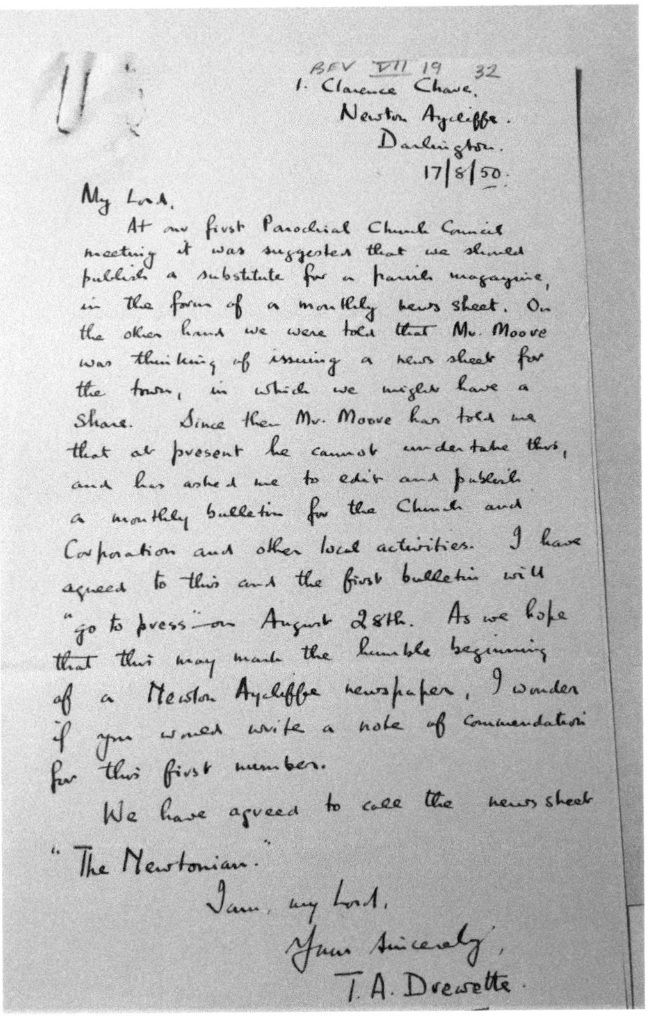

BEV VII 19 32
1. Clarence Chare.
Newton Aycliffe.
Darlington.
17/8/50.

My Lord,

At our first Parochial Church Council meeting it was suggested that we should publish a substitute for a parish magazine, in the form of a monthly news sheet. On the other hand we were told that Mr. Moore was thinking of issuing a news sheet for the town, in which we might have a share. Since then Mr. Moore has told me that at present he cannot undertake this, and has asked me to edit and publish a monthly bulletin for the Church and Corporation and other local activities. I have agreed to this and the first bulletin will "go to press" on August 28th. As we hope that this may mark the humble beginning of a Newton Aycliffe newspaper, I wonder if you would write a note of commendation for this first number.

We have agreed to call the news sheet "The Newtonian".

I am, my Lord,
Yours sincerely,
T. A. Drewette.

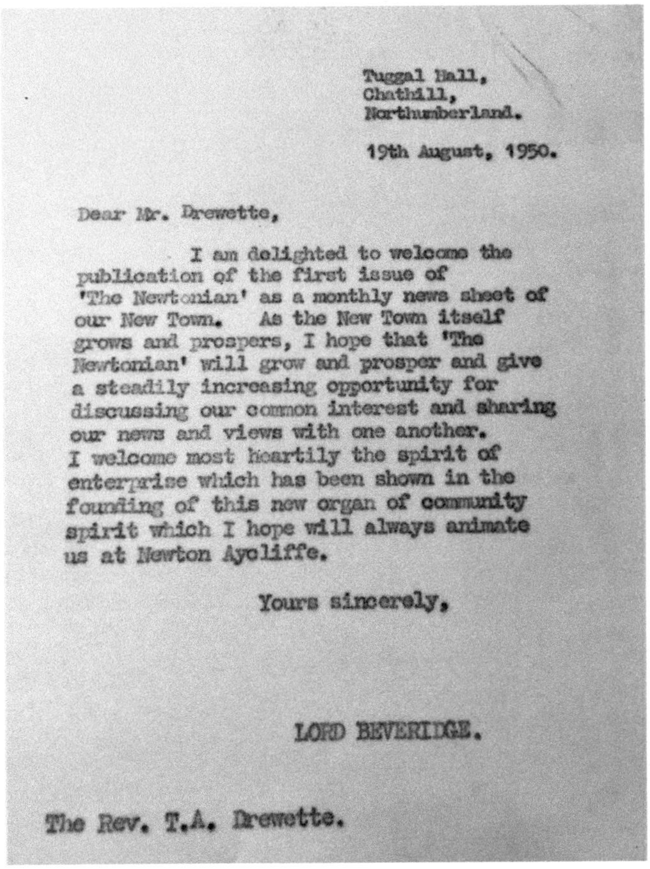

Tuggal Hall,
Chathill,
Northumberland.

19th August, 1950.

Dear Mr. Drewette,

I am delighted to welcome the publication of the first issue of 'The Newtonian' as a monthly news sheet of our New Town. As the New Town itself grows and prospers, I hope that 'The Newtonian' will grow and prosper and give a steadily increasing opportunity for discussing our common interest and sharing our news and views with one another.
I welcome most heartily the spirit of enterprise which has been shown in the founding of this new organ of community spirit which I hope will always animate us at Newton Aycliffe.

Yours sincerely,

LORD BEVERIDGE.

The Rev. T.A. Drewette.

Figure 51 - Letter from Reverend Drewette to Lord Beveridge and reply discussing the initiation of a town newsletter. (Photo courtesy the Beveridge Archive, L.S.E.).

Social Development

In February 1950 the Reverend Thomas Drewette was appointed to administer the Church of St. Clare in Newton Aycliffe. He was to become massively influential in the social development of this very young town. Rev. and Mrs. Drewette moved into No. 1 Clarence Chare at the beginning of May and he used a room at Clarence Farm as his first church on the town (opened on May 7th) with a glass fruit bowl as his font and borrowed furniture as its seating. The first baptisms on the new town occurred in May 1950. Clarence Farm also had a downstairs room used as a Reading Room.

Arguably his greatest accomplishment was to suggest that a town newsletter be written and circulated to all residents each month. On 17th August 1950 the Rev. Drewette wrote to Lord Beveridge suggesting the newsletter and that it be called 'The Newtonian'. Figure 51 shows the actual letter from Drewette to Beveridge and the reply from Lord Beveridge a couple of days later. 'The Newtonian' and subsequently 'The Newton News' have been published in Newton Aycliffe ever since. The newsletter was a labour of love described by the Rev. Drewette as having two functions: i) Informing residents of activities in the town and ii) Describing progress in the town and events so that they would be documented for historical purposes. Reverend Drewette assembled all the material (from many sources) and typed up the original. This was then passed to the Aycliffe Development Corporation where it was copied and distributed to residents every month. The first issue (Volume 1, No. 1) was issued on the 30th August 1950 (the September 1950 issue).

Figure 52 - The Clarence Farm Barn complex in a more recent photo showing the early Community Centre on the left and the two shops on the right. (Photo from Great Aycliffe Town Council)

Figure 53 - The first two shops in Newton Aycliffe – The Post Office and a General Grocery Shop (W. Duncan Ltd) – They occupied former cow byres at Clarence Farm. (Photo from Great Aycliffe Town Council).

The new residents of Newton Aycliffe quickly began putting together social institutions for the new town. On July 8th a children's sports day was held on Clarence Green and on July 10th the first Newton Aycliffe Post Office was opened in the Clarence Farm complex. The Reverend Drewette in his editorial in 'The Newtonian' (Vol. 1, No. 6) describes July 12th, 1950 as a 'memorable day' because that evening the first cricket practice was held which he interpreted as having begun the new town's sports club!

August was very busy - the Police Office at No. 1 Baliol Green (a small side building still present today) was opened, a Parish Church building fund was launched and on 17th August the converted barn at Clarence Farm was used as the Community Centre. The County Library was transferred into the Community Centre on August 21st and a public telephone became available on the 22nd.

The first edition of 'The Newtonian' appeared on August 30th 1950 edited by the Reverend Thomas Drewette. He continued to produce and edit 'The Newtonian' until 1955 after 55 editions.

During September the Community Centre came into full use. The rooms above the shops were also leased by the Community Association but required significant work to bring them into use. On the 4th September 1950 the Newton Aycliffe Football Club was inaugurated and used open space on the former ordnance range for training purposes. At a meeting of the Community Association they approved the Development Corporation's proposals for playing fields in the town. The Townswomen's Guild had its first meeting on the 18th September and on the 29th a troop of Boy Scouts was formed at Clarence Farm. Dressmaking and country dancing classes began on the 27th September and groups were formed for ambulance (first aid), darts and dominoes (Ernie Tennick ran the Darts and Dominoes Club – 2 shillings to join and 6 pence per week). The Youth Club transferred its activities from the Corporation Canteen to the Community Centre.

Figure 54 - Schindler-Gohner flats in Bede Crescent - some of the ones on the left formed temporary schoolrooms. (Photo courtesy Great Aycliffe Town Council).

October 1950 saw the beginning of the Tennis Club (in preparation for the following year) and the doctor's surgery opened. Later in October the doctor came into residence – Dr. Parker who many remember from their childhood – a large, seemingly gruff man who filled the surgery with cigarette smoke! Saturday November 4th 1950 at 2:30pm was the official opening of the Community Centre by Lady Beveridge. An Art Club was formed on the 13th and the first Film Night was held on the 16th November. The film nights were plagued with issues over the years (according to later editions of 'The Newtonian'), films failed to be delivered, video and audio weren't particularly good, even poorly behaved attendees were a problem! On the 24th November a 'sale of work' was held to raise funds for the Parish Church Building Fund.

The first school to open in Newton Aycliffe was a temporary arrangement of four flats in Bede Crescent that I think opened in 1950 and operated up to and after Sugar Hill opened in 1953. The school was at the left hand end of the block. The flats themselves were / are called Schindler – Gohner flats which were a form of prefabrication built and assembled by a Swiss Company.

As mentioned earlier the residents of the new town formed a Community Association relatively quickly in order to provide them with a voice in discussion with the Aycliffe Development Corporation. In August 1950, in a general meeting of the Community Association, they adopted the proposal that their management committee should explore the possibility of liaison with the Aycliffe Development Corporation.

This was forwarded to the Aycliffe Development Corporation in a letter and the response was friendly, but did point out that the Aycliffe Development Corporation worked for the Minister of Town and Country Planning and was simply charged with building the town per the Master Plan. They helpfully suggested that ideas and constructive criticism should be channelled through the Aycliffe Parish Council or the Darlington Rural District Council where the residents already had elected representatives. The Community Association responded that they simply wanted liaison with the Aycliffe Development Corporation, where early exchange of information could happen. This was the beginning of the development of the relationship between residents and their local governments.

Figure 55 - Durham District Services Bus No. D7 connecting Newton Aycliffe to Darlington in the 1950s.

Transportation was initially an issue for new residents. An early bus service from Newton Aycliffe to Darlington was run by the Newton Aycliffe Service Company, based in Darlington and owned by the Voy family. This family would subsequently run Central Coaches, a fondly remembered provider of coach trips throughout the 1960s and 1970s. The Northern/United No. 46 ran along the Great North Road from Darlington to Newcastle and stopped at the Gretna. The United No. 15 also ran along the Great North Road from Spennymoor to Darlington and the Durham District Services D7 ran from Darlington to the Bowburn area. These latter two were diverted into the new town and picked up at a variety of locations prior to specific routes being established. The Eden Bus Service connected Newton Aycliffe to Shildon and Bishop Auckland. Trains ran from Darlington to Bishop Auckland and Crook with a stop at Heighington Station.

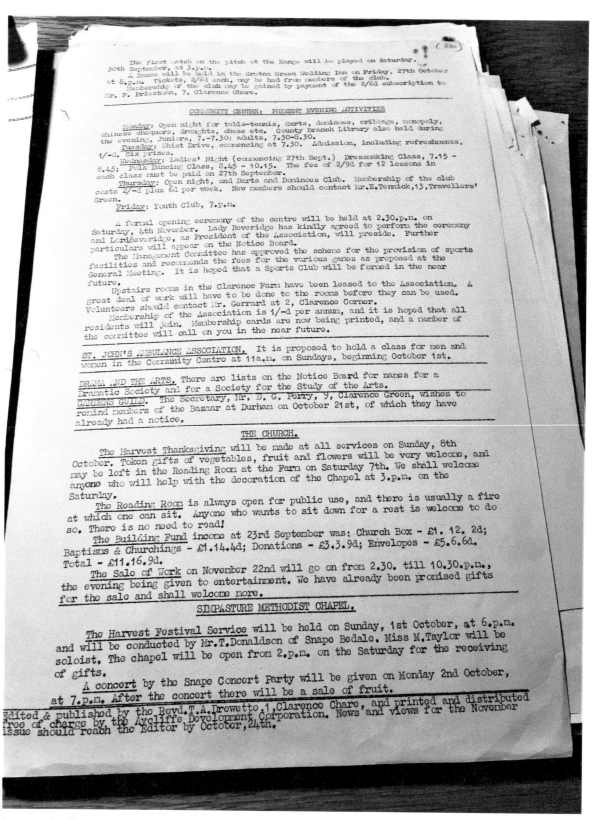

The first match on the pitch at the Range will be played on Saturday, 30th September, at 3.p.m.

A Dance will be held in the Gretna Green Wedding Inn on Friday, 27th October at 8.p.m. Tickets, 2/6d each, may be had from members of the club.

Membership of the club may be gained by payment of the 2/6d subscription to Mr. F. Priestman, 7, Clarence Chare.

COMMUNITY CENTRE: PRESENT EVENING ACTIVITIES

Monday: Open night for table-tennis, darts, dominoes, cribbage, monopoly, chinese chequers, draughts, chess etc. County Branch Library also held during the evening, Juniors, 7.-7.30: adults, 7.30-8.30.

Tuesday: Whist Drive, commencing at 7.30. Admission, including refreshments, 1/-d. Six prizes.

Wednesday: Ladies' Night (commencing 27th Sept.) Dressmaking Class, 7.15 - 8.45; Folk Dancing Class, 8.45 - 10.15. The fee of 2/9d for 12 lessons in each class must be paid on 27th September.

Thursday: Open night, and Darts and Dominoes Club. Membership of the club costs 2/-d plus 6d per week. New members should contact Mr.E.Tennick,13,Travellers' Green.

Friday: Youth Club, 7.p.m.

A formal opening ceremony of the centre will be held at 2.30.p.m. on Saturday, 4th November. Lady Beveridge has kindly agreed to perform the ceremony and Lord Beveridge, as President of the Association, will preside. Further particulars will appear on the Notice Board.

The Management Committee has approved the scheme for the provision of sports facilities and recommends the fees for the various games as proposed at the General Meeting. It is hoped that a Sports Club will be formed in the near future.

Upstairs rooms in the Clarence Farm have been leased to the Association. A great deal of work will have to be done to the rooms before they can be used. Volunteers should contact Mr. Gerrard at 2, Clarence Corner.

Membership of the Association is 1/-d per annum, and it is hoped that all residents will join. Membership cards are now being printed, and a member of the committee will call on you in the near future.

ST. JOHN'S AMBULANCE ASSOCIATION. It is proposed to hold a class for men and women in the Community Centre at 11a.m. on Sundays, beginning October 1st.

DRAMA AND THE ARTS. There are lists on the Notice Board for names for a Dramatic Society and for a Society for the Study of the Arts.

GARDENS GUILD. The Secretary, Mr. D. G. Perry, 9, Clarence Green, wishes to remind members of the Bazaar at Durham on October 21st, of which they have already had a notice.

THE CHURCH.

The Harvest Thanksgiving will be made at all services on Sunday, 8th October. Token gifts of vegetables, fruit and flowers will be very welcome, and may be left in the Reading Room at the Farm on Saturday 7th. We shall welcome anyone who will help with the decoration of the Chapel at 3.p.m. on the Saturday.

The Reading Room is always open for public use, and there is usually a fire at which one can sit. Anyone who wants to sit down for a rest is welcome to do so. There is no need to read!

The Building Fund income at 23rd September was: Church Box - £1. 12. 2d; Baptisms & Churchings - £1.14.4d; Donations - £3.3.9d; Envelopes - £5.6.6d. Total - £11.16.9d.

The Sale of Work on November 22nd will go on from 2.30. till 10.30.p.m., the evening being given to entertainment. We have already been promised gifts for the sale and shall welcome more.

SIMPASTURE METHODIST CHAPEL.

The Harvest Festival Service will be held on Sunday, 1st October, at 6.p.m. and will be conducted by Mr.T.Donaldson of Snape Bedale. Miss M.Taylor will be soloist. The chapel will be open from 2.p.m. on the Saturday for the receiving of gifts.

A concert by the Snape Concert Party will be given on Monday 2nd October, at 7.p.m. After the concert there will be a sale of fruit.

Edited & published by the Revd.T.A.Prewett,1,Clarence Chare, and printed and distributed free of charge by the Aycliffe Development Corporation. News and views for the November issue should reach the Editor by October,24th.

Figure 56 - The second page of scheduled events in Early Newton Aycliffe from The Newtonian, Volume 1, No. 2 (October 1950)

The emerging activities of residents of the new town are best illustrated by an example of the scheduled events from an early copy of 'The Newtonian' (Figure 56). The number of clubs and organisations would continue to grow throughout the 1950s.

Physical Growth

In May 1951 the Development Corporation, dismayed at the slow construction progress by contractors, sanctioned their own Direct Labour Department to undertake house building. This proved to be remarkably successful over the next few years. By 1953 the town consisted of 1000 houses and by 1955 they opened their 2000th house.

Within the Beveridge archive are a series of tabulations that include a list of businesses operating on the Trading Estate in 1951 (transcribed here as Appendix 2 and provided to Lord Beveridge by Mr. Sylph the Chairman of the North Eastern Industrial Estates Ltd.). It also contained a list of residents (as well as pending applications) by address in 1950 / 1951 and a list of workers by job type and salary. These data are tabulated here in Appendices 3 and 4. It is fascinating to see individuals on the list often before they had children, and when they were still young people with fairly junior jobs and seemingly impossibly low salaries. The last four pages of Appendix 4 include applicants for housing that had not yet been assigned. By the end of May 1951 there were 81 businesses with 2980 employees on the Aycliffe Trading Estate.

At a speech given by Beveridge on 7th June 1951 to executives and workers on the trading estate he outlined the points system to be used when assessing applicants for residence in Newton Aycliffe. Each applicant was given points based on a number of codes (A through I):

Code	Description	Points
A	Length of employment on Trading Estate	Six points for each year
B	Distance of travel to and from work	Two points for each mile (one way)
C	Wife's Employment	Ten points if employed on trading estate
D	Physical Disability	Maximum of five points if travel aggravated
E	Separation of Families	Five points if husband in lodgings and family elsewhere
F	Overcrowding	One point for each bedroom a family is currently short
G	Lack of separate home	Five points for family sharing home
H	Key Worker	One point
I	Special circumstances	To be decided by Housing Tenancy sub-committee - maximum ten points

Social Development

In 1951 a census-like compilation of residents (see Appendix 3, 4) indicated that rents for the Prefabs were £1 1s 1d per week.

In February of 1951 the Bishop of Durham visited the Clarence Farm Church of St. Clare's for the first time.

In December 1951 Miss E.M.B. Hamilton took up her position as Housing Manager for Aycliffe Development Corporation.

As a demonstration of their personal commitment to the social ideal of Newton Aycliffe, Lord and Lady Beveridge decided to move there. They lived at No. 5 Bede Crescent until late 1953. There are a series of letters between Beveridge and the then secretary of the Aycliffe Development Corporation, J.L. Moore discussing the 'fine detail' of their residence. At some point they had the Corporation carpenter build a set of shelves for his office, they asked if they could have the house 'knocked through' into No. 6 Bede Crescent to make it bigger (this request was declined) and they even took possession of the installed cooker after they left the property in 1953.

When they left the property there were extensive exchanges of letters to get the cooker packed and shipped as well as the shelving removed and re-cut to fit its new location in Oxford. Lord Beveridge donated his books to the Durham Library system and his office contents languished at the Aycliffe Development Corporation offices for some time before being shipped to him.

Interestingly, Lord Beveridge purchased two acres of land on the west side of Woodham Burn just north of Burn Lane (for £463 17s 5d) – he bought the land as a possible building site for a future home. He leased the land to a local farmer, Mr. Williams, for hay production and was ultimately persuaded to sell it to Mr. Williams by J.L. Moore because 'It now seems fairly certain that the New Town will never overspill the Burn in that direction' – Letter from Moore to Beveridge dated 16th July 1957.

A number of sources link Lord Beveridge to the large white house built at the end of Cumby Road. I have found no written indication that this house was in his plans, although some reference is made in correspondence to a new house called 'Acley'. Dr. Kerr and family ultimately occupied this house.

Figure 57 - The large white house at the top of Cumby Road – thought to have been built for Lord Beveridge but occupied by Dr. Kerr and family. (Photo from 'Tenants Handbook').

1952

Physical Growth

In 1952 the first purpose-built shops opened in Newton Aycliffe. These were in Ward 'A' and called Neville Parade. There were several shops underneath and flats above. Early occupants were: a bakery; Dewhurst's Butchers, a pharmacist; Pryce's Greengrocer; Stevens' Sub-post office; Brough's Grocers; Collinson's Hardware; a wet fish shop and a Co-Op. A bookmaker was up the stairs on the left in Figure 58. Laura Stevens had been selling cigarettes and confectionery from her home to builders and factory workers since 1937. In 1952 she was given the first shop at Neville Parade – Stevens'. Laura was also made the first sub-post mistress in the same shop.

Figure 58 - A very early picture of Neville Parade Shops – flowerbeds present (later removed because of vandalism), no phone boxes (1953 Tenants handbook).

Figure 59 - As in Figure 58 but a single phone box has been added (1952). The flowerbeds are still present. A second phone box and a stamp machine would be added later. (Reproduced by permission of Durham County Record Office, D/CL 5/1719).

Social Development

According to Boyes (2007) by 1952 the population of Newton Aycliffe was increasing rapidly and looking likely to exceed its 10,000 design-model and the Industrial Estate was struggling to find workers to fill the jobs available in the factories. The concern was that unemployed workers on Wearside or Teesside would be reluctant to relocate to Aycliffe if housing was not available due to slow building. In addition, competition for jobs from new I.C.I. developments at Wilton and Teesside would make workers reluctant to move to Aycliffe. However, the ongoing collapse of coal mining in southwest Durham created more unemployment and drove workers toward Aycliffe.

On the 21st and 22nd of May 1952 The Newton Aycliffe Dramatic Society put on a play entitled 'The Heiress' by Ruth and Augustus Goetz. The production was at the now ten year old Theatre at Aycliffe School at Copelaw and produced by Hugh and Dorothy Muirhead.

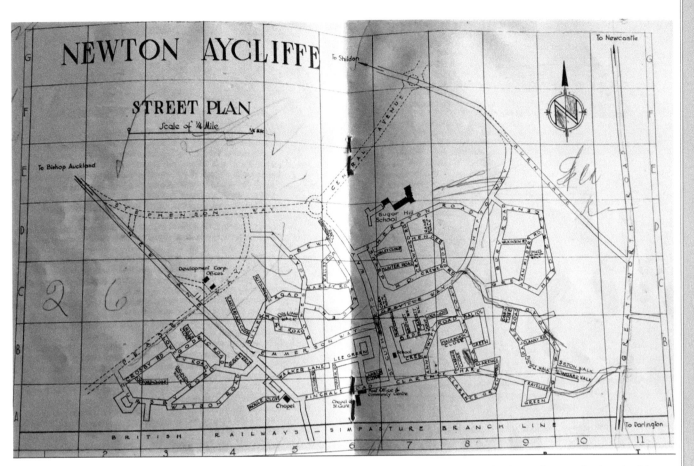

Figure 60 - The extent of Newton Aycliffe in 1953 (From the 1953 'Tenants Handbook'- the author apologises for his youthful scribble!)

Physical Growth

1953 was the first year the Aycliffe Development Corporation published a 'Tenants Handbook' designed to inform all residents of what was available in Newton Aycliffe as well as give advice on home care and gardening etc. The Handbook contained a town plan in its central pages describing the extent of Newton Aycliffe. The 1953 map still shows Burn Lane and New Lane (Clarence Chare) joined to The Great North Road and the town only extends to Sugar Hill School in the north and Pease Way in the west. (Figure 60)

The 'Tenants Handbook' described an overview of the early long-term plan for Newton Aycliffe. Today it reads like a bit of a dream scenario – the Town Centre was envisaged as containing 90 shops including department stores, a cinema, a residential hotel, offices, civic buildings, police station, community centre, health centre, library, General Post Office, banks, gas and electricity show rooms, two pubs, cafés and restaurants interspersed amongst them and other buildings. The Regional Hospital Board requested a site for a small general hospital and land was reserved on the north side of Central Avenue at its junction with The Great North Road. A Grammar Technical School was also contemplated at the Town Centre alongside Marlowe and Milton Hall Secondary Modern Schools. Sports fields were initially planned to be just north of the Town Centre.

Figure 61 - Sugar Hill Infants School immediately prior to completion in 1953. The Junior School on the left is not yet built.

In 1953 Sugar Hill Infants School opened and immediately relieved the pressure on the temporary school in the Bede Crescent flats. Since Junior School pupils also needed to use the Infants site at Sugar Hill, the Bede Crescent flats continued to be used. The Head of the school was Mrs. Milner and Mrs. Minnie Fryer was a much-loved teacher of many students in the 1950s and 1960s.

Toward the very end of 1953 the first purpose-built pub in the new town opened. The Iron Horse was a Vaux pub and opened on December 23rd 1953 on the site of Finchale Cottage Farm. It came complete with a large bowling green.

Figure 62 - The Iron Horse public house was the first purpose-built pub in Newton Aycliffe. It opened on Christmas Eve 1953. This photo from about 1955. Reproduced by permission of Durham County Record Office, D/CL 5/1718.

Social Development

The largest social event of 1953 was probably the Queen's Coronation and like most places, this was celebrated in Newton Aycliffe. The Aycliffe Development Corporation produced a souvenir program that illustrated their progress and ambitions in 1953 as well as the program of activities over several days. Originally planned for June 2nd the outdoor component was postponed until July 4th due to inclement weather. Activities included children's sports, a prize giving by Lord Beveridge, an award made to Lord Beveridge for his service to the town, some dancing, some singing and a fireworks display. These events were held on Sugar Hill Sports Ground.

In a letter from J.L. Moore (Secretary to the Aycliffe Development Corporation) to Lady Beveridge on April 1st 1953 he bemoans the need to suspend the planting of Coronation trees by children because of ongoing vandalism!

As part of the Coronation celebrations at 3:00pm on June 4th of 1953 the 1000th house to be built in Newton Aycliffe was opened. It was a rainy day and Lord and Lady Beveridge unveiled a plaque on the house at 2, Butler Road. This confirms the very rapid rate of construction required to house the influx of workers to the Industrial Estate. At 3:45pm on the same day an event took place at the 'Tunnel Road' where the first sod was cut by Mr. S.A. Sadler Forster (Chairman of the North Eastern Trading Estates Ltd) that began the tunnel underneath the Clarence Railway that would become the famous Blue Bridge.

The 1953 'Tenants Handbook' presents the 'Conditions of Tenancy' for life in Newton Aycliffe. Reading these in 2018 they sound very prescriptive, if not draconian! Living in Newton Aycliffe in the 1950s it didn't seem like life was so restrictive. However, a small note in an early edition of 'The Newtonian' did indicate that the Development Corporation were going to be issuing notice to tenants who had been repeatedly warned to tend to their gardens!

According to the 1953 Tenants Handbook there were two doctors offices in Newton Aycliffe and one dentist. Dr. Kerr had an office at 2 Bury Road and Dr. Parker had his office at 17 Finchale Road (next to the Community Centre). The dentist's office was upstairs at 17 Finchale Road. The dentist most people would remember from the 1950s and 1960s would have been Dr. Stafford however the 'Tenants Handbook' for 1953 lists a Mr. Nelson.

The 1953 'Tenants Handbook' also states that children who attended Secondary Modern School would go to the County Modern School for Boys or the Timothy Hackworth Modern School for Girls in Shildon. Some also went to Chilton Secondary Modern. Grammar School qualified children went to Bishop Auckland King James I Boy's Grammar or Bishop Auckland Girls Grammar School. Eden Bus Services transported all these children, with fares being refundable after submitting claim forms.

Maternity and Child Welfare was also complicated. The nearest facilities were at Chilton although the Community Association was hoping to host these appointments at the Community Centre. The nearest maternity home was at Hardwick Hall, Sedgefield but it was also possible to attend at Greenbank Maternity Hospital at Darlington. The nearest ambulance service was at Bishop Auckland.

1953

A small library was kept in a room above the Duncan's Shop on New Lane at the Community Centre and was apparently its most popular facility – it had previously been temporarily housed in one of the Prefabs.

Much of the 'Tenants Handbook' is devoted to helpful information on things such as home repair, gardening, home safety etc.

1953 was the year when the Welcoming Parties were initiated and many residents were introduced to each other as well as to the clubs and activities in the town. Miss E.M.B. Hamilton of the Housing department organised these get-togethers. Prior to this each tenant had been welcomed by a member of the Community Association, but as the rate of arrival increased, this became untenable.

On July 1st 1953 Lord Beveridge resigned his office as chairman of the Aycliffe Development Corporation and he and Lady Beveridge commenced their move from Bede Crescent to Oxford and Edinburgh. The subject of his resignation had been discussed in Parliament a year earlier. On 24th June 1952 an M.P., Mr. Dodd, had asked then Minister for Housing and Local Government Harold Macmillan if the removal of Lord Beveridge as chairman of Aycliffe Development Corporation could be reconsidered. Apparently there had been a strong reaction to his impending resignation. Dodd cited 'Does not the Minister appreciate that to millions of people he represents the best in public life?'(Parliamentary transcripts available at: www.hansards.millbanksystems.com).

'The Newtonian' continued to keep the town informed of the many events going on. An amusing announcement from The Garden's Guild in the July issue advertised 'sewage sludge' for sale at 2/6d a load (6 tons!!) – price reduced if you help load the wagon yourself!!!

On 17th May 1954 Don Vickers (as Chairman of the Community Association) presented his overview of progress and issues from the year 1953. It is clear that 'growing pains' continued and was, like all other New Towns, related to the lack of social amenities. The Association was doing well financially and spent money decorating the Clarence Farm Community Centre. It was recognised that a larger facility was required, but not a new central facility as initially proposed. The Aycliffe Development Corporation was able to produce a design for an extension to Clarence Farm that would cost £5000. This had not yet been brought forward to the County Council for funding. The location of the sports fields was also an issue in 1953. Originally sited near Sugar Hill (behind the modern 'town centre shops' I believe) the Aycliffe Development Corporation felt this land would be required for building. The cricket and football fields were therefore moved to the current Moore Lane site. The association also initiated a mid-week cinema and a maternity and child clinic at the Clarence Centre.

In late 1953 or early 1954 the 'Over Sixties Club' was initiated and proved to be quite popular. An early issue was the town demographic that was generally skewed to younger age groups.

1954

Physical Growth

The second part of Sugar Hill Primary School (the Junior School component) was completed and opened. The formal opening was on Friday, 26th November and Councillor J. Hudson performed the opening. Mr. D.H. Swan was the Headmaster and well-remembered teachers included: Mrs. Grice, Mrs. Bradley, Mrs. Pearson and Mr. Coxon.

The second group of local shops was completed in 1954 at Simpasture Gate (Ward 'B'). The shops were let to: Mrs. H. Batchelor, Middlesbrough (Grocery and Provisions), Mr. L. Coggins, Newbiggin-in-Teesdale (Greengrocery and Wet Fish), Mr. J.N. Holmes, Darlington (Butchery and Confectionery) and Mr. H. Cox, Newton Aycliffe (Newsagent, Sweets, Tobacco, Stationery and Hairdressing). In The Newtonian of April 1954 (Vol. 1, No. 44) the editor describes the proposed drapery and baby linen shop as not yet being let, but it was subsequently let to Mr. M. Hutchinson of Gateshead by June 1954. Mr. Coxs' gents' hairdressing shop beside Clarence Farm moved to Simpasture and the vacated shop became a ladies' hairdressers. The Community Association encouraged residents of Ward 'B' to sign a petition to lobby the Post Office to install a sub-post office at Simpasture.

Figure 63 - The almost complete Sugar Hill Primary School – the Infants School (left) was complete in 1953, the Junior School (right) was finished in 1954. This aerial photo is likely dated September 1954 with the Junior School almost finished. (Photo courtesy Great Aycliffe Town Council).

1954

81

Figure 64 - Newly built shops at Simpasture Gate (Ward 'B') – the shops are open and telegraph poles are still in place. Low Moor Farm in the background has not yet been demolished. Likely date 1954 – photo courtesy of Great Aycliffe Town Council.

Figure 65 - Newly built shops at Simpasture Gate (Ward 'B')- rare view toward Simpasture railway crossing – The single dark building beyond the shops is the early Methodist Church (Reproduced by permission of Durham County Record Office, D/CL 5/1721).

The second new public house probably opened sometime in 1954 - The Oak Tree was a Cameron's pub and built next to Neville Parade shops.

In June of 1954 Messrs. W. Coleman of Durham began the construction of St. Clare's Church that was expected to take one year to build. The general design was to resemble a barn as a nod to its more humble beginnings at Clarence Farm. The site of the church itself is almost exactly where Sugar Hill Farm once stood. Initially only the church plus a small, attached hall was to be built with a larger detached hall to follow. The total cost of the church was expected to be close to £40,000 and that would complete the church, the Parish Hall and the vicarage.

By October 1954, it was expected that construction would be beginning on the 38 shops in the Town Centre.

Figure 66 - The Oak Tree pub on the left with Neville Parade shops in the distance to the right. (Reproduced by permission of Durham County Record Office, D/CL 5/1722).

Social Development

In the early part of 1954, the Community Association, together with the Aycliffe Development Corporation, continued to host welcome parties for new residents. This allowed new people to meet each other as well as to become familiar with the many clubs and activities occurring on the new town.

In the August – September 1954 issue of 'The Newtonian' (Volume 1, No. 48) a comprehensive list of the social activities available to Newton Aycliffe residents was provided. This was obviously published to combat the growing sense that residents had limited opportunities for entertainment. The list is transcribed here:

Arts and Crafts, Brownies, Bridge Club, Church: Men's Guild, Men's Working Party, Mother's Union, Women's Working Party, Cubs, Cage Birds, Cake Decoration, Chess, Chrysanthemum Society, Country Dancing, Dressmaking, Enquirer's Club, Football Association, Rugby Association, First Aid, Girl Guides, Gardens Guild, Labour Party, Library, Methodists Homemakers Class, Methodists Women's Fellowship, Male Voice Choir, Music Society, NSPCC, Over Sixties Club, Painting Club, Poetry Club, Photography Club, Catholic Women's League, Catholic Women's Sewing Club, Red Cross Society, Scouts, Townswomen's Guild (Choir, Drama, Social Studies), Tropical Fish, Tennis, Table Tennis, Whist, Workingmen's Club, Women's Club, Youth Club, Dramatic Society, Dancing (Ballroom and Children's Classes).

The Newton Aycliffe Dramatic Society presented a play called 'A Murder Has Been Arranged' by Emlyn Williams. The play was presented at the Aycliffe School Theatre, Copelaw on the 6th May 1954 and buses were arranged from Neville Parade to Copelaw. Reginald P. Ekins and W. Swanwick produced the play. It is interesting to observe that advertisements in the program now come from shops at Neville Parade as well as Darlington and surrounding communities.

1954

In the October quarter of 1954 the first weddings are recorded in St. Clare's Parish.

In the August – September edition of 'The Newtonian' it was announced that the Parish Council had approved the £5000 for the new, expanded Community Centre at the Clarence Farm area (later to be called 'The Beveridge Hall').

Figure 67 - The Puncheon wedding couple outside St. Clare's Church, Clarence Farm. (Photo from Chapman, 1995)

1955

Physical Growth

The second 'Tenants Handbook' was published in 1955.

On the 21st January 1955 the new 'Beveridge Hall' was opened by Mr. Hugh Dalton M.P. and became a component of the 'Beveridge Centre' which included the converted Clarence Farm outbuildings. The new hall was designed by Goldstraw and Associates and built at a cost of £5000. Don Vickers praised the design in his annual report as chairman of the Community Association dated 31st March 1955.

The new Church of England of St. Clare's was completed in 1955. The movement of St. Clare's Church to its new premises provided additional space for the Community Centre. The Reverend Thomas Drewette was very involved with the design and figure 68 shows his sketch of the altar area that he provided to the architects.

In November 1955 Lady Beveridge made a donation of £25 1s 10d to pay for the new processional cross that had been purchased and that she was very taken with (see Figure 71).

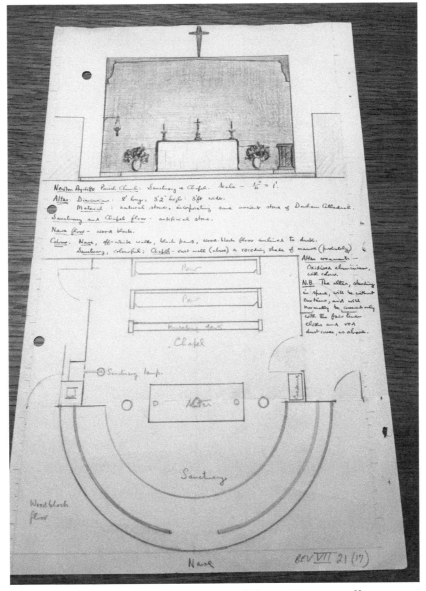

Figure 68 - Hand drawn sketch by the Reverend Thomas Drewette of how the area around the altar in the new St. Clare's Church should be configured. Drewette sent this copy to Lord Beveridge for review. (From Beveridge Archive, L.S.E.)

Figure 69 - St. Clare's Church as originally built in 1955 with a small attached church hall on the left. (Photo from St. Clare's 25ᵗʰ Anniversary Brochure).

The author remembers attending Wolf Cubs in the small hall prior to the later new hall being built. Choir practice was also held in the small hall.

As part of the construction of St. Clare's Church a vicarage was built and still stands today. The dedication ceremony of St. Clare's Church occurred on 9ᵗʰ July 1955 and is shown in Figure 71.

Figure 70 - The newly built vicarage at St. Clare's. This allowed the Reverend Tom Drewette to move from No. 1 Clarence Chare. The Workingmen's Club and Church Close are not built yet. (Photo from St. Clare's 25ᵗʰ Anniversary Brochure).

Figure 71 - Photo taken after the dedication ceremony of St. Clare's Church on the 9th July 1955 by the then Bishop of Durham Michael Ramsey. Rev. Tom Drewette is on the far right, the processional cross, bought by Lady Beveridge is held by the person on the far left. (Photo from the 25th Anniversary Booklet)

As children at Sugar Hill School it was very exciting to watch the Town Centre being constructed behind the School Field.

In March 1955, the 2000th house was opened in Newton Aycliffe and apparently the 1000th house built by the Corporation's Direct Labour Department was also built.

Figure 72 - The northern portion of the Town Centre shopping area on Beveridge Way. Photo dated 1955. (Reproduced by permission of Durham County Record Office, D/CL 5/1690).

Social Development

In the annual report of the Community Association the Chairman, Don Vickers stated that there were at least 22 regular events at the Community Centre as well as additional casual events. He estimated that 2700 people per week made use of the Centre. When the new expanded hall was opened on 21st January, a dance was held that evening – demand for entry was high and 100 people were turned away! This highlighted the Community Association's problem of trying to keep up with Newton Aycliffe's rapid growth.

The February 1955 issue of 'The Newtonian' was Volume 2, No. 1 and began the tenure of Mr. N. Blackburn as editor. His first editorial praised his predecessor Tom Drewette who had edited the paper since September 1950.

It is interesting to observe that an article in February 1955 begins to discuss the issue of too many cars without garages on the new town – a problem that we all still live with in 2019! Apparently 330 garages already existed on the town but these were not enough. This problem was magnified in 1955 because the law prevented any vehicle being parked on the highway at night without lights – fines were being issued! In the April issue of 'The Newtonian' it is announced that a series of laybys would be opened to allow cars to be parked overnight without lights. These were to be in Baliol Green, Lee Green, Dixon Road, Bede Crescent, and Bury Road (where there would be two).

In April 1955 it was announced that the Chairman of the Community Association, Don Vickers, had just been appointed as a Justice of the Peace for County Durham and the editor of 'The Newtonian' congratulated him.

At 4:00am on April 19th 1955 a loud explosion occurred in the new resin plant at the Bakelite factory. The explosion broke windows as far away as Heighington and Redworth and injured 10 employees, some of whom were hospitalised for several months. The extent of the blast damage was reduced by the presence of residual 'blast berms' between the buildings. These were earthen mounds that were a legacy of the prior life of these buildings as part of the ROF 59 ammunition factory.

In May 1955 'The Newtonian' announced the names of Sugar Hill scholars who had qualified to attend County Grammar schools: Vivienne Blackburn, David R. Brown, Patricia Cody, Margaret E. Gerrard, John E. Gooding, Roy G. Simpson, Francis R. Tweddle and Robert R. Wise. The girls were scheduled to go to Spennymoor Grammar School and the boys to The King James I Grammar School in Bishop Auckland. These were some of the children who had moved to the town as youngsters.

In the summer of 1955 the Community Association held its annual Sports Day. Although chilly, the weather was fine and over 1000 residents attended. The event included a police dog demonstration, sideshows, refreshments, sporting events etc.

The new sports fields at the junction of Burn Lane (later to be called Moore Lane) and the Great North Road were being prepared in 1955 and was expected to be ready by spring 1956. Fresh grass had been seeded and people were cautioned to 'keep off'!

In the August 1955 edition of The Newtonian an advertisement occurs in which Ernie Tennick of 19, Clarence Chare looks to sell Kennel Club registered Boxer puppies for £10 10s 10d each. The author can remember going into the Tennick's kitchen and seeing these puppies in a box at age 3.

On December 23rd 1955 The Iron Horse pub opened its upstairs buffet bar on the second anniversary of the pub itself opening.

1955

1956

Physical Growth

In 1956 the final step was taken to directly link Newton Aycliffe to the Trading Estate that had spawned its existence. St. Cuthbert's Way was extended southwards under the Clarence Railway which was supported overhead by the now famous Blue Bridge. This endeavour came at a cost of £200,000. Since 1956, the Bridge has been at least two shades of blue and was actually grey for a number of years!

Figure 73 - St. Cuthbert's Way is extended under the Clarence Railway and Newton Aycliffe is linked to its Trading Estate. The famous Blue Bridge supports the railway. (Photo from 1956 and courtesy Great Aycliffe Town Council).

In the four corners of the bridge are stone carvings (see Figure 74) representing the See of Durham, the Royal Ordnance Factory, Newton Aycliffe's initiation in 1948 and the building of the bridge in 1956. A Time Capsule was placed behind one of the carvings. Its actual location and contents are a secret but are held in an envelope in the 'Artefacts Cabinet' in the Great Aycliffe Town Council chamber. It is scheduled to be opened in 2038.

Figure 74 - Carvings associated with the Blue Bridge to commemorate significant events associated with the New Town.
Top Left - See of Durham   *Top Right - Newton Aycliffe 1948*
Bottom Left - Building of the Blue Bridge 1956   *Bottom Right - Royal Ordnance Factory*

Initial construction continued on the Town Centre and the first shop opened sometime in late 1956 according to the 1957 'Tenants Handbook'. Construction also began on The Newton Aycliffe Modern School that would become Marlowe Hall Secondary Modern. The Working Men's Club opened part-way through 1956, next to Sugar Hill School at the corner of St. Cuthbert's Way and Sheraton Road. The National Federated Brewery Ltd. financed it.

Figure 75 - The Working Men's Club in its original form, no second story, no large concert hall. (Photo courtesy of Great Aycliffe Parish Council)

Social Development

In his annual report to the Community Association, Don Vickers again expressed the growing concern that the location of the Beveridge Community Centre, on the southern fringe of the town, meant it was becoming increasingly isolated from the growing population to the north. Also the facilities in the Beveridge Hall area were now stretched to capacity – a bigger facility with more flexibility and located at the Town Centre was recommended. The estimated cost was £25,000, with annual operating costs of £2500 per annum.

There is an acknowledgement that the cinema (films showing in the Beveridge Hall) is their most criticised area. Children and some adults were noisy, seats were uncomfortable, films were not new and the whole effort was expensive. The committee knew that their cinematic efforts must improve because it was already apparent that an actual cinema was not going to come to Newton Aycliffe. The provision of a larger screen television was not as successful as hoped. Don Vickers also took time to commend Miss Hamilton for organising the welcome parties that she had been running for three years.

1956

The visit of a Miss La Touch who apparently provided comptroller oversight on groups that received public funds happened late in the year. The Community Association was in receipt of 'gifts-in-aid' and therefore needed auditing – nothing was anticipated as being 'amiss'.

In this annual report Don Vickers announced that he would not be seeking re-election as Chairman after six years of service.

On Tuesday March 20th 1956 the Newton Aycliffe Dramatic Society performed a comedy in three acts by Talbot Rothwell called 'Queen Elizabeth Slept Here' now at the Beveridge Hall Theatre.

With the opening of the new road through the Blue Bridge into the Trading Estate there was much anticipation of buses having consistent routes through the town that would allow bus shelters to be built to provide shelter for waiting passengers.

In the January 1956 issue of 'The Newtonian', the editor broaches for the first time the question as to whether residents will, at any time in the future, be able to buy their council houses.

The editor of 'The Newtonian' highlighted two lingering issues for the New Town in January 1956. The two issues were 1) rents being high relative to older towns in the area and 2) the difficulty predicting the ultimate population of Newton Aycliffe. The rent issue had been discussed since the inception of the new town – according to the Development Corporation rents were higher because the quality of the homes was higher than most local colliery houses. This was true however an additional reason was that the capital costs involved in constructing a new town from scratch needed to be reflected in the rental income.

The population predictability was a thorn in the side of the Community Association because their primary task was providing services to the residents and it was difficult to scale requirements to a fluid population prediction. In the March issue of 'The Newtonian', the rent cost issue came to a head. The Corporation announced that building costs and interest rates had been rising and rents must also rise to accommodate this. Apparently the law required the Corporation to issue each resident with a 'Notice to Quit' with a letter offering a new tenancy at the increased rent. According to the announcement the majority of rents would rise between 6 pence and 2 shillings and 6 pence with a few rarely up to 4 shillings and 6 pence.

In July 1956, the Parish Council were informed that the concrete tank structures at the Baliol Green playground were being used as toilet facilities and were very unsanitary. It was proposed that they be demolished and removed. As a child that regularly played at this playground I remember those 'smelly' structures well. It was probably a year or two after this item in 'The Newtonian' that they were finally knocked down.

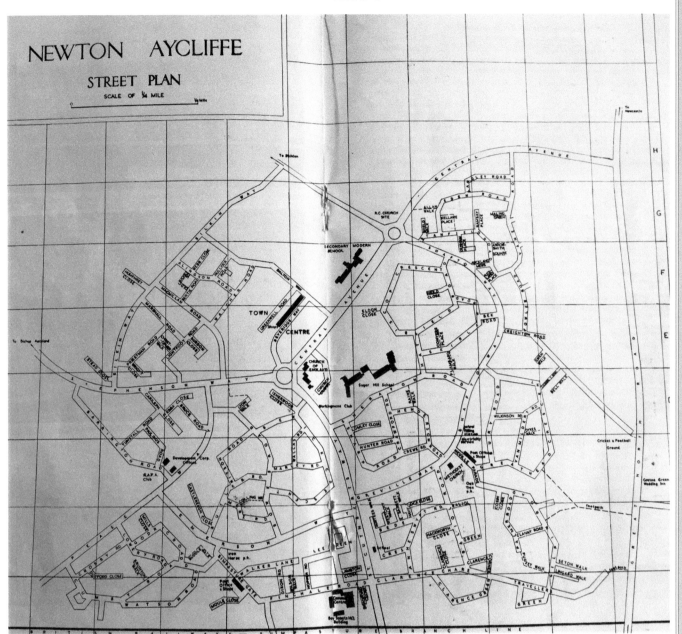

Figure 76 - The extent of Newton Aycliffe in 1957 (From the 1957 Tenants Handbook)

Physical Growth

In 1957 the Ministry of Housing and Local Government came to the realisation that Newton Aycliffe's low housing density was inadequate and the estimated final population estimate was raised from 10,000 to 20,000. This was linked to the unexpectedly rapid jobs growth shown by the Industrial Estate. A new Master Plan was drafted calling for 6 wards with about 3000 people per ward. The concept of each ward having some shops, green spaces, childcare facilities etc. was maintained.

The third 'Tenants Handbook' was published in 1957.

Work continued on the Town Centre during 1957 with a completed row of shops on the north side of Beveridge Way shown on the map from the 'Tenants Handbook'.

The construction of The Newton Aycliffe Modern School (to be called Marlowe Hall Secondary Modern School) was completed in 1957. Alderman W. Baines of the County Education Committee formally opened it on Thursday the 7th November 1957. Mel Harland remembers first attending Sugar Hill Junior School and then Shildon all boys school for a year before entering Marlowe Hall as part of its first student intake in 1957.

Social Development

1957 was a bit of a watershed year for public opinion on the progress of the new town social experiment. In March 1957, The Daily Express delivered a bombshell. Merrick Winn, in an article entitled 'The Town That Has No Heart', described Newton Aycliffe as 'perfect planning and perfect monotony . . . nothing to do and nowhere to go.' Most of all, he criticised the town centre: 'twelve small shops, a few more half-built, and a keen, cold wind' (few shopkeepers were prepared to set up in an empty town and wait for customers to move in). This began a long running media campaign to denigrate the concept and reality of Newton Aycliffe and other new towns.

The new chairman of the Community Association (J. Stanworth) was in the unenviable position of presenting the first annual report in which the Association actually lost money! A loss of £500 was made in 1957. Apparently, the discussion of a new community centre at the town centre was held yet again (it had happened annually for several years) with no resolution. The appointment of a Full-Time Warden to the Community Association was announced and named as a Mr. Sheridan. The appointment also came with a house to rent that apparently influenced his decision! In August 1957 Miss La Touch's White Paper was published and favourable to the affairs of the Association.

Mr. Stanworth announced that 'The Newtonian' was to be published in a new form because the numbers involved were now too large for the Development Corporation to handle. A printing company would produce it and be paid from advertising revenue.

Concern was expressed that the level of vandalism at the Community Centre was increasing with one fifth of the seats unserviceable. Legal action would have to be considered. The annual sports day was another success, although the weather was cold and windy.

Figure 77 - Initially called "The Secondary Modern School" it was quickly renamed "Marlowe Hall Secondary Modern School" (Reproduced by permission of Durham County Record Office, D/CL 5/1689)

Physical Growth

On Thursday 3rd July 1958 the then key shop in the Town Centre shopping complex opened – F.W. Woolworths at number 30, Beveridge Way. The shop would quickly become a haven for children choosing toys and sweets.

Marlowe Hall Secondary Modern School was completed and opened in late 1957 and freshly occupied in early 1958.

On the 6th December 1958, 'The Newtonian' contained an aerial photograph showing the extent of Newton Aycliffe. This is shown in Figure 78.

Social Development

The July 1958 issue of 'The Newtonian' was Volume 3, No. 1 and was the first under the new editor C.A. Sheridan (the third editor after Drewette and Blackburn). It was also the first printed edition changing from a typed document that was reproduced and distributed. Longer articles, clearer typeset and more professional advertisements characterise the newssheet. All these reflect the continued growth of Newton Aycliffe from a pioneer community to fully-fledged town.

The most significant announcement in 'The Newtonian' Volume 3, No. 1 was that the Corporation would now make any of their housing stock available for sale to tenants. The Corporation was also prepared to advance mortgages to suitable purchasers. In addition the Corporation offered land 'on the Woodham Burn site' for people who wished to build their own houses. This was a significant break from the original social ideal of Newton Aycliffe.

The Parish Council discussed plans for the new Simpasture Playing Field complex. It would include four tennis courts, practice cricket wickets, two football fields and a children's playground.

Figure 78 - The extent of Newton Aycliffe 1958. (Aerial Photo courtesy of Aycliffe Development Corporation via The Newtonian)

The 1st Newton Aycliffe Boy Scout Hut was burned down and then subsequently looted for wood and contents. 'The Newtonian' expressed outrage at this work of vandals.

The Newton Aycliffe Youth Club was apparently on hard times because of a lack of adult leadership. Sergeant Pearson stepped up to help and things began to improve. The Club did well in the Bishop Auckland and District Sports Meeting, held on the evening of Thursday 5th May 1958. They won the Junior Boys 4 x 110yds relay (David Appleby, Noel Sturdy, Robert Martin, Christopher Allen), the Junior Girls 4 x 110yds relay (Ann Bolton, Sylvia Sperrings, Pat Bushby, Carole Browne), the Girls 75yds (Ann Bolton), they were second in the Boys 75yds (David Appleby), First in the Boys High Jump (Noel Sturdy) and second in the Girls High Jump (Carole Browne).

New club start-ups include: the Camera Club, The Astronomy Club, the Cycling Club, and the Rambling and Field Clubs.

The Dancing Academy announced the results of Medal Test Examinations for Ballroom, Ballet, and Tap. In addition they announced that Linda Knight and Alan Close were awarded a Silver Cup 1st Prize at the N.C.O.T.A. annual modern ballroom dancing competition in Wallsend on May 27th 1958.

The University of Leyden in Holland sent 17 students to study the great social experiment that was Newton Aycliffe where the students attended a welcoming party, interviewed local inhabitants and stayed with local families.

The children's section announced the formation of The Loco-Spotters Club (a very popular pastime at the Steam – Diesel transition of this time) and was looking for an adult to lead the activity.

The Newton Aycliffe Community Association annual sports day was held on June 21st 1958 at the Sugar Hill School field.

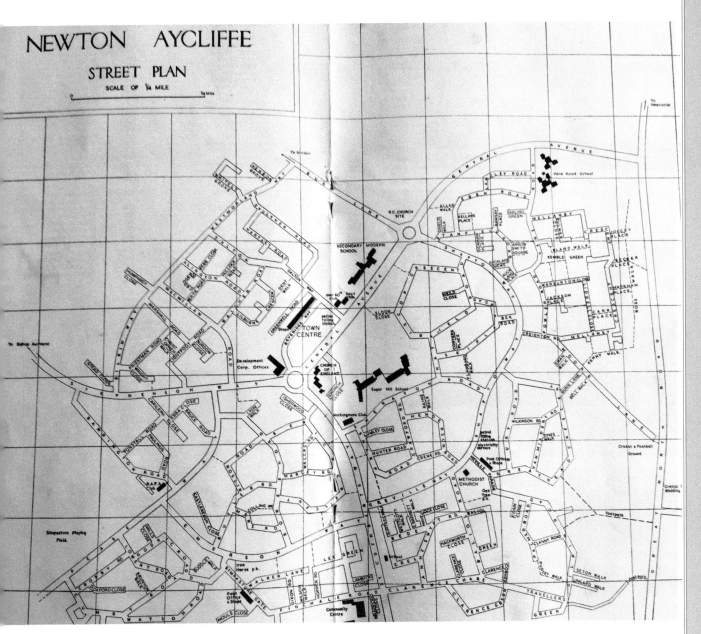

Figure 79 - The extent of Newton Aycliffe in 1959 (From the 1959 'Tenants Handbook')

Physical Growth

The fourth 'Tenants Handbook' was published in 1959. The included town plan shows the completed Vane Road school and the new church hall at St. Clare's.

Looking at various aerial photographs it seems that Churchill House at the Town Centre was completed in 1959 / 1960 along with the row of shops attached to it. It was a great novelty at the time to hear the new town clock chiming out every quarter of an hour. In fact it became very important to local children to be able to monitor the time whilst wandering / playing around the town. The additional strip of shops on the north side of Beveridge Way was shown on the earlier 1957 town plan.

Vane Road Primary School opened at the junction of Vane Road and Central Avenue.

Figure 80 - The Town Centre under construction, Churchill House looks complete with the Clock Tower and bells that would become a feature of the town - ringing each quarter of an hour. (Photo from Great Aycliffe Town Council).

Figure 81 - Vane Road Primary School (Reproduced by permission of Durham County Record Office, D/ CL 5/1681)

The new Methodist Church was completed and opened at the Neville Parade site with the opening and dedication scheduled for 3rd January 1959. Lord Beveridge was scheduled to perform the opening and appears on the printed program. However, circumstances prevented him travelling up from Oxford and the church was actually opened by Lady Starmer from Darlington.

Figure 82 - Cover of the Program for the opening of the Neville Parade Methodist Church, erroneously showing Lord Beveridge as performing the ceremony. It was actually opened by Lady Starmer from Darlington because Lord Beveridge was suffering from arthritis.

Figure 83 - Churchill House and the Town Centre Clock Tower (about 1960) – note the elaborate, flower covered roundabout in front. (Reproduced by permission of Durham County Record Office, D/CL 5/1685)

Social Development

On the 17th March 1960 the then Secretary / Warden of the Newton Aycliffe Community Association Mr. Sheridan, presented a summary of events that the Association participated in from March 1959 to March 1960. This report announced that the Association had organised the town's first Festival – a full week with a Sports Day and 30 shows. The only lament was that takings were modest but positive. It seemed that the Community Association was barely solvent throughout this time.

A number of new clubs were also set up in 1959: The Angling Club, The Gun Club, The Town Band, The Jazz Club, and a boys section of the Red Cross. Apparently the most successful venture in terms of numbers involved was the Youth Coffee Bar Club. The Skating Club was formed and in only five nights it generated income of £17 10s 0d and canteen sales of £12. Apparently numbers were increasing rapidly and much fun was had every Saturday night.

The Community Association continued to recognise that as the town grew the Beveridge Hall Complex (on the southern edge of town) became increasingly far from the centre of the towns' population. They continued to recognise the need for a new Community Centre in the Town Centre area.

Lord Beveridge was clearly contemplating selling his two acres of land on Burn Lane. He had previously turned down an offer of £300 from Mr. Williamson (adjacent farmer) and on the 11th May 1959 he asked J.L. Moore (Secretary to the Aycliffe Development Corporation) to provide him with a summary of what he had paid for the land – he had paid £463 17s 5d.

1960

Physical Growth

According to the January 1961 edition of 'The Newtonian', 308 houses were completed during 1960, despite the year being characterised as having almost continuous rain! These houses were located mainly behind the Town Centre and adjacent to Vane Road and Fowler Road where 170 houses remained to be completed. Good progress was also made on 51 houses adjoining Pease Way and 222 houses from Burn Lane toward the Great North Road.

The Town Centre continued to expand with 11 shops and a bank (presumably Barclays) being built on the south side of Beveridge Way and six also being added on the north side. All were either open for business or awaiting the installation of shop fronts.

An additional secondary modern school commenced construction near Marlowe Hall – this was Milton Hall Secondary Modern School and was expected to open in early 1962. The Fire Station and Ambulance depot on Central Avenue were also nearing completion.

The Roman Catholic Church and presbytery were opened at the junction of Burn Lane and Central Avenue. The Working Men's Club added its large concert hall in 1960/61. The R.A.F.A club also opened next to Pease Way in former Development Corporation offices and the Queen opened the Boys' Club during her visit. Apparently the new private housing development on Woodham Burn was also off to a good start with all plots in Phase 1 being sold.

Figure 84 - St. Mary's Roman Catholic Church (Photo courtesy Great Aycliffe Town Council)

One disappointment was that construction of the Health Centre and Library complex on Dalton Way had been delayed but contracts were now being let and construction would begin shortly.

Social Development

Possibly the most memorable event of 1960 was when Queen Elizabeth and Prince Philip visited the New Town on 27th May of that year. The author has a memory of being eight years old and taken from Sugar Hill School and lining the short access path to Marlowe Hall Secondary Modern School to wave flags as the Queen entered the school. In addition my mother Eva Creaney worked in the kitchens at Marlowe Hall and recalled learning to curtsey for when the Queen passed by.

In 1986 Harry Bilton had the following memory of this event: 'May 27th.1960 was a very happy day for everyone in the new town. We had been looking forward to the visit of Her Majesty Queen Elizabeth and His Royal Highness Prince Philip for some time and the excitement in the town was intense. Although I was employed by Aycliffe Development Corporation, it was in my capacity as part-time Clerk to the Great Aycliffe Parish Council that I was lucky enough to be presented to Her Majesty and Prince Philip, at Simpasture Playing Field. I was so overawed by the occasion that I cannot recall the conversation, but it will live in my memory for ever.' (Taken from the BBC Reloaded project).

Figure 85 - The Queen visiting Newton Aycliffe in 1960 – on her way into Marlowe Hall Secondary Modern School (Photo from Chapman, 1995).

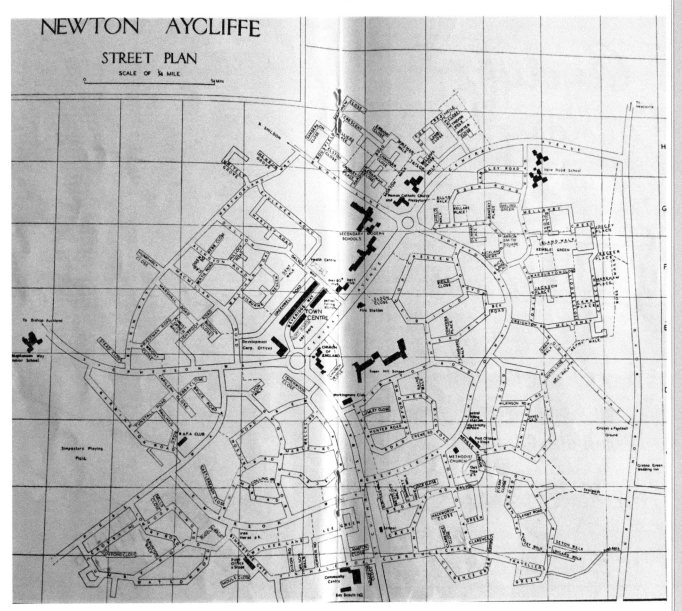

Figure 86 - The extent of Newton Aycliffe in 1961 (From the 1961 'Tenants Handbook')

Physical Growth

During 1961 the Development Corporation built 337 houses completing houses near Vane Road, Pease Way and Burn Lane.

The fifth 'Tenants Handbook' was published in 1961. This was to be the last one distributed to all residents. The sheer numbers and the cost made universal distribution prohibitive so future copies only went to new tenants.

The Post Master General announced that there would be a Crown Post Office in the Town Centre. However, their intention was to close the Sub Post Offices at Simpasture and Neville Parade, a move that was not approved by the Parish Council.

Figure 87 - The newly built British Legion Club (Reproduced by permission of Durham County Record Office, D/CL 5/1673)

In 1957 a group of ex-servicemen had got together to establish a local branch of the British Legion and in 1961 the British Legion facility opened in Macmillan Road. It lasted until 2015 when it released its association with the Royal British Legion due to onerous dues and renamed itself 'The Phoenix Club'.

Milton Hall Secondary Modern School continued construction and was expected to be open by Easter 1962. Mr. Leslie Soulsby was appointed the first Headmaster in December 1961.

The young demographic of early Newton Aycliffe presented difficulties of overcrowding in primary schools and in September of 1961 the catchment areas for Sugar Hill and Vane Road schools were adjusted to alleviate overcrowding at Vane Road. The Vane Road overcrowding persisted into 1962 when 62 pupils were accommodated in the Methodist and St. Clare's Church halls. Many recall being in class sizes of 40 students at Sugar Hill in the early 1960s.

Figure 88 - The new church hall at St. Clare's Church (on the right). (Reproduced by permission of Durham County Record Office, D/CL 5/1684).

Figure 89 - The Working Men's Club adds a large concert hall. This coined its local name "The Big Club".
(Reproduced by permission of Durham County Record Office, D/CL 5/1683)

The Fire Station on Central Avenue was built, but not opened until October 1961, because there were no local houses for the firemen – this took about three months to fix with a row of houses on Central Avenue adjacent to the Station. The formal opening took place on 1st November and was performed by County Councillor G.A. Yews.

In September of 1961, a figure arrived on the New Town who would become very familiar to residents. Mrs. E.M. Lincoln became The Salvation Army representative and would be seen around the town for years to come.

The Industrial Estate continued to grow – an additional 150,000 square feet of space was added in the current year with 167,000 square feet planned for the following year. Over 500 jobs were added in 1961 with the same amount expected in 1962.

Figure 90 - A view of the relatively new Town Centre taken from the top of the Clock Tower (probably early 1961) – nearest building is Barclays Bank. Circular things in the foreground were short-lived concrete flowerbeds. (Photo courtesy of Great Aycliffe Town Council).

Social Development

By February of 1961, the Community Association was in somewhat desperate financial condition according to that month's 'The Newtonian'. It was stated that expenses were £3000 per year, which left them with a £300 deficit. An appeal was launched to try and raise funds. A meeting was held on the 27th April 1961 and the second resolution was to dissolve the Community Association. That resolution was carried. The Association had helped most recreational organisations on the Town at one time or another since its formation in January 1949. In the July issue of 'The Newtonian' the formation of the Newton Aycliffe Council of Local Organisations (NACLO) was announced to handle the organisations previously handled by the Community Association.

At the end of 1960, a Tenants' Association was formed to facilitate liaison with the Development Corporation. Its formation appears to have been linked to a need for a means of relating to the non-elected Development Corporation. By the end of 1961 the Association had 250 members and had resolved a number of issues for tenants. They had concerns about 3 particular areas: i) The dispatching of arrears notices without any consideration of tenants previous good payment history, ii) The lack of policy on house exchanges and transfers and iii) Tenants moving in to houses that have not been cleaned properly.

On March 12th the B.B.C. broadcast its Sunday Half Hour program from the new Methodist Church in Newton Aycliffe.

In the April edition of the Newtonian the ever-present spectre of teenage vandalism was again a significant topic. According to the Editor it resulted from the end of National Service leaving youths with too much free time, apparently a significant target was the street-lights that were being shot from air rifles.

A contributing factor was likely the high number of children in the demographically 'young' town combined with insufficient organised activities to occupy them.

In mid-summer the Working Men's Club announced that the Tuesday evening teenage dance would cease – the reason given being vandalism, fighting and generally bad behaviour by a small minority. This was something of a reputation that dogged teens from Newton Aycliffe during the 1960s and 1970s.

Throughout the late 1950s and into the early 1960s it seemed that attempts to keep a weekly cinema going on the town were failing. Cinemas in adjacent towns (Darlington, Bishop Auckland) were closing. The impetus to build an actual cinema in Newton Aycliffe (instead of showing films in the Beveridge Hall) was also waning. This was all probably related to the concurrent rise of accessibility to television.

On April 6th 1961 one of the town's early leadership figures, the Reverend Tom Drewette passed away. The May issue of the Newtonian eulogised this giant among early pioneers of Newton Aycliffe who died far too young at 49.

In July 1961, the Parish Council announced that it regretfully accepted the resignation of Clerk to the Parish Council, Harry Bilton – apparently on medical grounds. I recall that Harry had a heart attack while gardening at around this time.

The Townswomen's Guild held its 11th birthday party on December 4th and said farewell to one of their founder members and their chairman from 1950 to 1959, Mrs. Morton (wife of Andrew Morton the town's chief horticulturist).

Towards the end of 1961, a law was enacted to penalise individuals who allowed their dogs to foul the pavement (another ongoing Newton Aycliffe problem). A scheme was also started to allow disabled people to park their vehicles closer to shops (quite innovative for the time).

Figure 91 - The Church of Jesus Christ of the Latter Day Saints (early 1960s) – (Reproduced by permission of Durham County Record Office, D/CL 5/1694)

Figure 92 - Stephenson Way Primary School, probably 1963 (Reproduced by permission of Durham County Record Office, D/CL 5/1676)

1962

Physical Growth

The Church of Jesus Christ of the Latter Day Saints was completed at its site on Shafto Way. A number of missionaries from the U.S.A. assisted with construction.

In 1962 the Development Corporation completed 300 houses in the area bounded by Burn Lane and Central Avenue. Apparently many of these were built for sale or lease. An additional 400 houses were in various stages of construction by the end of 1962.

Also in July 1962 a modern style supermarket opened in the Town Centre - Fine Fare. This was from a chain of supermarkets that began in Welwyn Garden City. The company was sold to The Dee Corporation in 1986 and re-branded as Somerfield/Gateway. Additional work in the Town Centre was suspended because the Corporation recognised that the volume of car traffic had become so large that it had become necessary to pedestrianise the central area and have car parks on the flanks. Apparently the Ministry of Town and Country Planning were considering this proposal.

The later (1963) Hailsham Report which suggested raising the town's population to 45,000 required a complete re-think of the Town Centre layout and work was suspended for several months.

Shafto House old peoples home was under construction on Shafto Way.

Milton Hall Secondary Modern and the Roman Catholic Primary School also opened in 1962. Milton Hall opened after the Easter break with 216 pupils transferred from Marlowe Hall. Its capacity was 450 pupils.

Construction started in 1962 on Stephenson Way Primary School and the Territorial Army headquarters in Greenwell Road (the Parish and District Councils had both voted against this location since it is dominantly residential). The Parish Council started work on the Cemetery and the Moore Lane playing fields after having approved the variously discussed layouts.

There was a brief discussion by the Council in 1962 over the construction of a swimming baths, but this expenditure - and a projection that it would run at a significant loss - dissuaded everyone. At that time children travelled to the swimming baths in Gladstone Street, Darlington for lessons and recreation.

Social Development

In March 1962 the Parish Council voted to petition the County Council to confer urban status on the Great Aycliffe Parish (Newton Aycliffe, Aycliffe Village and the Industrial Estate). Apparently the choice was move to urban status or remain under the wing of Darlington Rural District Council. As things stood the New Town was paying about 60% of the rates etc. into Darlington Rural District but only had 33% of seats on that council. There was also a suspicion that an unfair distribution of spending across the RDC was heavily disadvantaging Newton Aycliffe. This appeal was ultimately declined.

They also announced that the Parish Council offices at Churchill House would no longer operate a six-day week and would be closed on a Saturday.

In the February issue of 'The Newtonian', the editor continued his lament that there was insufficient hall and facility space on the New Town to accommodate all the children – apparently the Boys and Girls Club was full and only half of applicants were members.

Also in February a large advertisement appeared in 'The Newtonian' placed by the Aycliffe Development Corporation and offering houses for sale – new houses in Burn Lane as well as any other Corporation house currently being rented. In Burn Lane a new semi-detached, 3 bedroom house with no garage was £2800 and a larger, detached, 3 bedroom house with garage was £3650 – these prices seem minuscule by 2018 standards!

On August 11th the first Newton Aycliffe Show was held at the new Moore Lane Sports Club – although 3000 people attended, the Moore Lane Sports Club lost £70 on the venture. On August 22nd the Newton Aycliffe Amateur Operatic Society held its inaugural meeting at the Methodist Church hall. In September 1962, the Great Aycliffe Sports and Athletic Association was formed, to administer the new playing fields at Moore Lane.

1963

Physical Growth

The winter of 1962 / 1963 was particularly bad – very cold with high snowfall recorded. This brought building work on the new town to a standstill for ten weeks. During 1963, the Development Corporation completed only a total of 191 houses with another six privately built. A further 173 houses were under construction at the end of 1963. Work also started on the roads and sewers in the South West area where 1050 houses were planned.

On April 1st 1963 all but two of the Aycliffe Development Corporation resigned. Those who left were Mr. C.S. Robinson (who had replaced Lord Beveridge as Chairman), Mr. W.N. Davis, Mr. A.J. Alsop and Mr. T.J. Cahill all of whom were original members of the Corporation from 1947. The only two members who didn't resign were J.R.S. Middlewood and C.U. Peat. It seems likely that this was linked to the merging of Aycliffe and Peterlee Development Boards into a single body by the Government.

In November 1963 Lord Hailsham presented a study of conditions in the north east of England. This led to a government white paper that emphasised that the Darlington/ Aycliffe area would be the focus of future industrial and population growth. This would compensate for job losses in the coalfield to the northwest where mines were played out and closing. In fact most of the mines in South West Durham were closed by 1968. The government felt that this made population expansion at Newton Aycliffe inevitable and asked the Development Corporation to raise the planned final population from 20,000 to 45,000. This required an areal expansion and the area to the northwest of the current designated area seemed optimal.

In 1966 an area of 1643 acres was added to Newton Aycliffe's Designated Area via an amendment order. This kind of proposed increase in population would require adjustments in scale to the Town Centre and this was also discussed. In addition The Hailsham Report (1963) also announced the creation of a third new town in County Durham – Washington New Town.

The Health Centre facilities at the Town Centre opened on 18th September 1963 and were called the Newton Aycliffe School Clinic and Maternity and Child Welfare Centre. In addition the Library opened on the same site. The primary school on Stephenson Way opened, as did the aged persons home at Shafto House on Shafto Way. A sub-Post Office was opened at the Town Centre pending a decision to open a Crown Post Office in the same area.

At the beginning of 1963 the Industrial Estate had 5000 workers. The growth of jobs on the Trading Estate continued with several factories expanding as well as new site approvals for additional factories for G.E.C. (a 50,000 square foot factory initially employing 1500 skilled and semi-skilled workers), Yardley's Ltd., R. Cripps Ltd, S.A.B. Brake Regulator Co. Ltd. plus others. In July 1963 Eaton's (which started on the town as E.N.V. in 1950) announced a further expansion of 100,000 square feet that would take the factory to 260,000 square feet and would add 300 jobs.

Figure 93 - The second generation of small bungalows that replaced the original, first generation prefabs in Clarence and Travellers Green. This photo was taken in 2018 as the bungalows were being vacated ready for demolition.

In 1963/1964 it was determined that the original Prefabs had outlived their design life – they were found nationally to be corroding at a series of key welding points. It was proposed that they be demolished and 'normal' council houses built. However, the residents so loved their Prefabs that they lobbied the Aycliffe Development Corporation and the replacement bungalows were built in the image of the originals. Since some residents would be returning to new bungalows on the same site as their Prefab some effort was put in to preserving their gardens. Eventually 38 bungalows replaced Prefabs and the remaining three Prefabs were simply demolished. The three vacant sites were combined with some adjacent vacant land and 11 houses and garages were built in the triangle formed by Clarence and Travellers' Greens and the Clarence railway.

As I am writing this book (2018) these second generation bungalows are being emptied ready for demolition and to build new housing on the site. So the original Prefabs lasted 15 or 16 years and the second generation ones lasted 54 years.

In the July 1963 issue of The Newtonian a teenaged Brenda Green made a heartfelt appeal to the youths of the town to find activities to keep them occupied over the summer rather than cause mischief!

The cemetery on Stephenson Way was completed in 1963 with the earliest interment being the death of Frances Regan on 14th December 1963 according to the online inventory of burials maintained by the Great Aycliffe Town Council. On a personal note the author's best friend of the time was killed in a road traffic accident on the Great North Road (crossing on his bicycle to go trainspotting) and was buried in Newton Aycliffe cemetery in May 1964.

The December 1963 issue of 'The Newtonian' announces for the first time that Santa Claus will be given a tour of the town on Christmas Eve. This appears to be sponsored and implemented by the Territorial Association. These tours have persisted as a Newton Aycliffe event since this time and are still running today. An early Santa Claus was Harry Bilton. The growing size of the town has seen an increase up to eight different Santa routes in recent times.

In 1963 the Clarence Railway finally closed. For a time many coal trucks were parked on the abandoned line. The old rail bed is now part of the Great Aycliffe Way.

Chapter Six

The Remaining 1960s

By 1964, the original Community Association was defunct according to The Newtonian.

On the 15th May 1964 Edward Heath (then Secretary of State for Trade and Industry) opened a 26,000 square foot factory for SAB Brake Regulators as the Industrial Estate continued to grow and provide jobs to the local community. A further expansion was announced in early 1970.

In May 1964 the Great Aycliffe Parish Council announced that funding was in place to develop playing fields at Moore Lane. Councillor Donald Vickers commented that it was about time the town had such a recreation facility.

The week of June 7th - 13th 1964 saw the first Carnival Week to be held in Newton Aycliffe. It came with a fairground and a parade and began an institution that lasted for many years.

In August 1964 Woodham Burn was analysed as having water so polluted that it was declared unfit for human consumption. This simply added to a regional water pollution issue with Demon's Beck covered in foam (and called informally the 'stinky beck') due to draining Newton Aycliffe's sewerage plant as well as the industrial estate. These streams fed the River Skerne that ultimately drains into the River Tees. The Skerne was extremely polluted by the upstream Fishburn coke works as well as the Aycliffe Trading Estate and made the River Tees the most polluted river in Europe during this time.

In the autumn of 1964 children who were deemed to have passed the 11-plus (the examination was abandoned that year) entered a new Grammar School – Ferryhill Grammar Technical School. These children formed the 1st form at Ferryhill and children from local Secondary Modern Schools (including Marlowe Hall) filled years 2 through 4. Children were taken by bus from Newton Aycliffe with various pick-up points throughout the town. The bus that picked up at the Beveridge Hall on Finchale Road also collected in Aycliffe Village, Heighington and Redworth before heading to Ferryhill – a trip that took about an hour. This arrangement worked well enough that it curtailed earlier plans to build a Grammar School at the town centre.

As mentioned earlier a parliamentary report was released in 1966 that suggested that Newton Aycliffe's population should rise to 45,000. As a result, an extra 1643 acres of land on the northwest side of Woodham Burn was added to the 'Designated Area'. In April 1968 the Corporation was granted a compulsory purchase order to also incorporate Middridge into the Designated Area for Newton Aycliffe.

The status of the New Town (as viewed by the Aycliffe Development Corporation) is comprehensively described in The Reports of the Development Corporations (1967) – pages 5 – 32. The report was developed based on the new projected population of 45,000 and therefore appears now to 'overstretch' itself in terms of planning.

Figure 94 - The Williamfield and Redhouse areas showing the much higher density, flat roofed housing that led to people calling Newton Aycliffe 'Matchbox City' (Photo courtesy Great Aycliffe Town Council)

A plan to relocate the Town Centre to the other side of Woodham Burn (to make it central to the 45,000 person New Town) had been presented and rejected. Preliminary discussions with Shildon UDC on the incorporation of Middridge into the Designated Area had begun. Construction of houses was occurring in Williamfield (by private contractors) and in Elmfield by the Corporations Direct Labour Department. Sadly, the Direct Labour Department was only constructing an average of 264 homes per year in the 1960s. Applications for development had been submitted for Redhouse, Horndale, Williamfield and Burnhill. Many former residents will remember the installation of smokeless fuel appliances in response to the Clean Air Act (1956) – the first 984 of these were installed by March 1967.

The Aycliffe Industrial Estate continued to develop and in 1967 had a total of 8620 workers. The older wartime buildings were being demolished and vacant sites put up for tenancy. A training centre with 72 places was scheduled to open in September 1967 and would draw trainees from most of southern Durham.

In the late 1960s the Town Centre was pedestrianised with parking placed behind the shops along Central Avenue.

In April 1966, 'The Newtonian' announced the impending resignation of Miss E.M.B. Hamilton from the Aycliffe Development Council. There had been a premature release of this information in February that was then rescinded in the March issue.

On the 2nd July 1968 an enormous thunderstorm struck the town and a lot of surface flooding occurred.

The Southerne Club opened on Hawkshead Place prior to 1970.

In October 1969 'The Newtonian' became 'The Newton News' (having transitioned through 'The Newtonian News') and began to be issued twice a month.

In the mid 1960s, The Great North Road, a mainstay of local Newton Aycliffe connectivity was bypassed as the A1(M) was pushed through County Durham. The former A1 was redesignated as the A167 and traffic load dropped considerably. The town remained connected to the new motorway network via the junction at Coatham Mundeville.

Sometime in the mid-1960s, one Antoni Imiela moved to Newton Aycliffe and quickly became one of the most notorious criminals associated with the town. A number of petty crimes led to him spending time in Borstal as a child and eventually he was given seven life sentences for rapes and sexual assaults he committed as the 'M25 Rapist'. He died in March 2018, at age 63 in HMP Wakefield.

Chapter Seven

The 1970s

Figure 95 - Woodham Comprehensive just prior to opening (photo from The Newtonian, 6th December 1969 issue)

The 1970s began with a scandal involving T. Dan Smith who was chairman of Aycliffe and Peterlee Development Corporation from 1968 to 1970. He was apparently involved with the firm of Poulson architects and acting as a public relations man for them throughout the north. He was eventually charged and convicted of accepting bribes (£156,000 +/-) and sentenced to six years in prison. He only served three years. His conviction had nothing to do with Newton Aycliffe but his former job as Chairman of Aycliffe and Peterlee Development Corporation caused significant negative PR for the two towns.

In The Newtonian dated the end of June 1970 the headline read 'Please, Don't Knock Williamfield' obviously a reaction to negative commentary on this newest part of the town. Apparently the 'boxy' houses, the high density of them and the distance from the town centre were all strong negatives. In addition there were considerable problems with the construction of these houses – flat, leaky roofs, drafty and they required considerable rehabilitation almost immediately.

On October 4th 1970 the St Francis Church / School in Horndale was formally opened. The Rev. Martin King was commissioned as priest with special responsibility for the project. The school was a joint operation between the Church of England and the Methodist Church. It opened to children on November 9th and the first Head teacher was Mr. Joe Bainbridge quickly followed by Mr. Ian Stage.

In November 1970 the owners of the Aycliffe Stock Car Stadium were first notified that when their lease was finished in two years time they would have to vacate for the building of new factories. However the stadium endured until 9th November 1989 when the need for prime industrial land eventually caught up with it. It had opened in the late 1940s possibly as a greyhound track then a Speedway training track and finally a Stock Car track in 1954. Many residents and former residents recall watching the racing at the circuit on the south side of the Trading Estate. At the very least residents recall the roar of the relatively un-silenced motors!

In December 1970 a folk singing club 'The Candlelite Folk Club' met at The Oak Tree pub. Also in 1970 the Labour Club was completed and Woodham Comprehensive School opened.

In early 1970 construction of the infamous ramp in the centre of Beveridge Way began. Across the summer of 1970 shops began to open 'up the ramp' including moves from other premises for Fred Bainbridge (hairdresser) from a small shop on Greenwell Road and Harry Harding (toy store) who moved to the largest shop at the top of the ramp.

In November 1970 a formal notice of name change appeared in 'The Newton News' announcing that Marlowe and Milton Hall Secondary Modern Schools were merged to form The Avenue Comprehensive as education in the U.K. continued to evolve. The actual merger may have occurred as early as 1967.

In 1971 the lakes at Simpasture were developed and many residents of that time fondly remember renting boats and spending time paddling around in them. In November 1971 Dennis Stevenson, aged only 26, was appointed Chairman of the joint Aycliffe and Peterlee Development Corporation. In his tenure from 1971 to 1980 he was regarded as very forward thinking bringing a dynamism to the office that promoted the popularity of the two towns.

On November 27th 1972 another pub – The Dandy Cart – was opened in Newton Aycliffe according to 'The Newton News'.

Toward the end of 1972 'The Newtonian' (strangely renamed back again from being 'The Newton News') reported that a private housing development on 25 acres at School Aycliffe was under way. Forty-nine houses were completed in phase 1 and another 49 were contemplated for phase 2 with 42 plots already sold. The selling of Corporation houses to sitting tenants was going well with 229 sales completed and a further 312 in progress. Houses were priced at a 20% discount on market value. 'The Newtonian' even provided articles on obtaining mortgages and general advice around house purchase.

In 1973 the Aycliffe Development Corporation was given control of the Industrial estate and began a vigorous campaign to attract more business. In the 5 years to 1978 an additional 50% of factory space was added and an additional 24 companies attracted. At the end of the seventies the Trading Estate had 10,000 employees in a number of diverse, internationally connected companies. The Corporation began advertising Newton Aycliffe in the national press with the slogan 'Newton Aycliffe – Where Ideas Grow' in an attempt to attract further jobs to the area.

The mid 1970s weren't generally a good time for quality of life in the U.K. – ongoing industrial action and a general downturn in the economy made things increasingly difficult. The Newtonian discussed the prospect of petrol rationing later in the year – the economic downturn seemed to make the 25th Anniversary celebrations of Newton Aycliffe's creation more subdued in November. A dinner dance for 200 people was hosted by the Round Table (with Syd Howarth as its Chairman) and a multi-denominational church service was held. Proceeds from the dinner dance were eventually used to provide a swimming hoist for disabled swimmers at the Recreation Centre in March 1975.

On April 1st 1974, the Parish Council was re-designated 'Great Aycliffe Town Council' and the first Mayor was Mrs. Win Dormer with her 17 year-old daughter Christine as her Mayoress. The town passed from the control of Darlington Rural District Council to Sedgefield District Council and an immediate rate rise was incurred. This seems to have been the beginning of some significant animosity amongst Sedgefield District Council, Durham County Council and Great Aycliffe Town Council.

A broad sweep through 'The Newton News'/ 'The Newtonian' articles of the 1970s suggests a lot of this was in fighting related to the apparent industrial success of Newton Aycliffe compared to the older industrial areas of Sedgefield District and County Durham in general. At this time Garry Phillipson became Chief Executive of Aycliffe and Peterlee Development Corporations (see his book, Phillipson (1988) for details of his time in that role).

The 1970s saw a number of facilities built and added that enriched the lives of Newton Aycliffe residents. Greenfield Comprehensive School opened in 1974 and has evolved over the years to provide focused education to local students. In 2000 it was designated as a specialist Arts and Science College and in 2015 took over the facility at Shildon Sunnydale to provide a dual site facility. In 1973/1974 the Recreation Centre was built and opened on the 24th July 1974 with a sports hall and a swimming pool. The initial plan in 1970 called for a twin cinema, banqueting facilities, new shops and a theatre but the finance was only sufficient for the sports hall and swimming pool. It even attempted to offer a separate cinema service but lack of public interest caused it to close in 1977.

On 31st January 1975, 'The Newton News'/ 'The Newtonian' described the visit of World War Two air ace, Douglas Bader to the Training Centre on the Industrial Estate to present awards.

Figure 96 - Aycliffe Leisure Centre (Photo courtesy of the Newton News)

Later in 1975, residents of 90 houses in Hawkshead Place and then 92 houses in Horndale, had to be temporarily moved out because of issues related to damp rising through the concrete floors. Apparently these houses were built by the Development Corporation's own housing department and a waterproofing compound was omitted from the concrete mix.

On August 31st 1975 the world celebrated the 150th anniversary of steam trains on the Stockton and Darlington Railway. A cavalcade of 30 steam trains ran from Shildon to Darlington, passing through Newton Aycliffe. Attendance at this event was huge, with 10,000 parking spaces being created on the Industrial Estate and spectators packing all areas where a view could be obtained. In another railway related item – in 1978 a 'halt' (unstaffed platform) was opened to allow Newton Aycliffe residents to access the train system on the Darlington – Bishop Auckland line without hiking up to Heighington Station.

As 1975 closed, Dennis Stevenson provided his Christmas message on behalf of Aycliffe Development Corporation and highlighted the fact that 400 families had moved into Newton Aycliffe and new factories were constantly being added despite the general downturn in industry nationwide.

On Saturday January 10th 1976 Dennis Stevenson opened the new Meeting Hall at Greenfield as the towns rapid expansion continued. In February 1976 Union Carbide announced an expansion that would generate 500 new jobs, a trend that continued through 1976.

By February 1977 Aycliffe had hit a record level of employment with 6791 men and 2349 women employed on the Trading Estate. This was a 10% increase since 1970 during a time when national unemployment increased by 8%. By the end of 1978 the total employees exceeded 10,000. During the 1970s Newton Aycliffe began advertising more widely for both industry and skilled workers including campaigns in the U.S.A. and Scotland.

In 1976 Elmfield Primary School was re-opened after a fire destroyed it in the early hours of February 1st, 1975. It would finally close on August 1st, 2007. It began its new life with a modified purpose and would be used for community events, as well as schooling, during the day. The Burnhill Boys Club (October 5th) and the Rotary Club also opened in 1976 and the Municipal Golf Course opened a year later.

On the 22nd May 1976, Lilian Holmes laid the foundation stone of a second Methodist Church in Newton Aycliffe. Lilian had been associated with Methodism on the town since it started prior to the town's inception. On the 11th December 1976 the Burnhill Way Methodist Church was opened on the Agnew Estate.

Towards the end of 1976, Harry Bilton provided a brief history of the St. Clare's church bell that had been in use for 25 years since 23rd December 1951. Apparently it weighed 2 cwt. and came from H.M.S. Prosperpine. Lord Beveridge, through contacts at the Admiralty, had facilitated its purchase for £18 1s 5d (including shipping!).

1977 did not start well. On January 9th, the town's biggest fire-related tragedy occurred when five members of the Kitching family lost their lives. The parents, a grandmother and a younger sister and brother were all killed. Apparently two surviving children went to live with relatives in Essex and an elder surviving sister moved in with her boyfriend's parents. The Mayor's fund raising effort eventually raised £3913.03 for the family.

The year 1977 was the Silver Jubilee anniversary (25th) of the Queen's ascension to the throne and Silver Jubilee street parties were held across the country. This was also true in Newton Aycliffe and 'The Newton News'/ 'The Newtonian' was filled with articles to stir patriotism throughout the year. The Jubilee Committee ended up with a small surplus of £104.68 which it passed on to the Boy Scout hut fund and a pensioners' fund. On September 24th 1977, an open air rock/pop concert was attempted with local band the Mynd headlining. The concert was staged at Cobbler's Hall but sadly only attracted 450 people.

In May 1977 a new vicar was appointed at St. Clare's Church – Granville Gibson. He was also later appointed as Chairman of the Board of Directors of Aycliffe Community Radio. This proved to have been a dark time for the church, as he was later arrested in 2014 for historic sexual offences. He was convicted in 2016 of two sexual offences against young men while vicar of St. Clare's from 1977 to 1985 and sentenced to one year in prison. As late as July 9th 1995, he had been invited back to St. Clare's for the 40th anniversary of its opening. In July 2019 he was convicted of an additional offence and given a 10-month jail term.

An advertisement appeared in 'The Newton News'/ 'The Newtonian' on the 24th February 1978 for detached houses built by Bovis in 'The Chase' for a price 'from £15,495'. The late 1970s was a time of significant inflation and within months the price on these same houses had gone up to £16,495.

The Oakleaf Complex was formally opened on May 31st 1978 by Prince Charles at the former site of Simpasture Farm. He conducted the opening as well as visiting the local radio station – Aycliffe Community Radio. The radio station was initially proposed in January 1978 but it was thought that Sedgefield District Council would not approve. However, the efforts of station manager Harry Rowell and his volunteers eventually got it operating by May 1978.

The Town Centre continued to evolve and Boots opened a large shop in 1978 and the Fine Fare supermarket announced they would build a £2.1 million 'superstore' with car park. On March 23rd 'The Cubby' (a gathering place for older people) opened next to the library and in April M.I.N.D opened a club to help people deal with mental health issues. 1978 was also when a mini-roundabout replaced the large one at the town centre (causing some driver confusion and significant citizen outrage!), the Gretna Green Wedding Inn opened the 'Inn Cognito' – Newton Aycliffe's first night club and Durham County Council began to think about reducing Newton Aycliffe's target population from 45,000 to 34,000. Sedgefield District Council began to contemplate removing the possibility of tenants buying their houses and also planning to cut the construction of new council houses in Newton Aycliffe in favour of repairing houses in older communities in Sedgefield District.

In 1979 an open-air market began in the pedestrianised Town Centre – officially opened on October 2nd at 11:30am by the Chairman of Sedgefield District Council.

Also in 1979 the Mayor's robes were presented to the Town Council by the crew of HMS Eskimo to mark the occasion of HMS Eskimo receiving Freedom of the Town.

The Aycliffe Development Corporation began to modify its approach to its housing stock. Throughout the 1950s, the vast majority of houses were Corporation owned but the new Labour government of the 1960s realised that the lack of opportunity to buy housing was contributing to a net migration out of the town. Then there began a concerted effort to sell housing stock into private hands. The 1970s saw considerable progress as home ownership approached 20% by 1974. After 1976 Old Age Pensioners were provided with free extra insulation to curtail their energy costs (in the face of a global energy crisis). A project was announced in July 1977 that would replace the flat roofs on many of the newer houses with normal, pitched roofs as well as new waterproofing on many in Williamfield and Redhouse. Crudens Ltd originally built these houses in 1967 and 1968 from a Swedish prototype. This was funded at £300,000 initially and designed to overcome the newer part of the town's reputation as 'matchbox city'. This was announced as completed in January 1978.

On the 30th June 1978 the Aycliffe Development Corporation transferred its housing stock to Sedgefield District Council. This precipitated a major philosophical shift away from the social, 'classless society' model of the late 1940s and 1950s.

Private contractors were allowed to build new housing estates (Byerley Park, The Chase, and Woodham Village after 1981) and in 1979 they contemplated selling council houses to sitting tenants again. This followed a survey to sense tenant interest in house purchase that resulted in 1000 expressions of interest.

By the end of the 1970s new housing had been added in Horndale, Byerley Park, The Chase, Burnhill, Cobbler's Hall and Agnew areas and the town's population was nearing 28,000.

During the 1970s Newton Aycliffe was twinned with the Swedish town of Perstorp based on a link between the towns mayors and the purchase of Bakelite / BXL by the Perstorp Company.

In early 1979 the Aycliffe Development Corporation put the rents of their Town Centre shops up by four or five times. Ravenseft Properties owned the shops on the Woolworths side of Beveridge Way and they put their rents up by up to nine times. These rent increases precipitated the closure of some shops in the Town Centre and probably triggered the difficulties the Town Centre would have in the eyes of residents.

On the 30th March 1979, Doctor Parker retired. He was the town's first doctor and many of us who were children in the 1950s recall attending his surgery at 17, Finchale Road. He had moved to the Medical Centre at the Town Centre for the latter part of his career.

Significant elections were held in May/June of 1979 and for the first time a party other than the labour party – the Aycliffe First party – held a majority on the Town Council. Their leader Jill Frise became the new mayor. This situation lasted about a year until an odd coalition of Labour and Conservative councillors ousted Aycliffe First in all committees and for Mayor.

On August 21st 1979 Patrick Mower (a T.V. celebrity) opened the new Fine Fare Superstore at the Town Centre. The opening of a 26,000 square foot modern supermarket with associated car park heralded the era of modern shopping into Newton Aycliffe.

The 1970s finished with Newton Aycliffe pushing to get 'District' status that would have placed budgetary control in the town's own hands with limited outside interference. Sedgefield District Council expressed deep scepticism at this attempt to take further control into the hands of Newton Aycliffe. Sedgefield also expressed a desire to build on the open 'greens' in the older part of the town to accommodate aging residents.

Throughout the 1970s, articles and letters appear in 'The Newton News'/ 'The Newtonian' consistently referencing vandalism on the town as well as 'smells' (from unknown sources) that permeate the town. The smells were variously attributed to the sewerage plant near Aycliffe Village or factories on the Trading Estate (particularly Chemical Compounds, later Great Lakes Chemical Co.).

During the 1970s residents of Newton Aycliffe fondly recall the famous 'Carnival' characterised by a parade with many floats from organisations in the town, jazz bands, athletic events, a fairground and the 'Miss Newton Aycliffe' competition. The parade generally 'mustered' at Baliol Green and then progressed up to Shafto Way, Central Avenue, Stephenson Way, and Pease Way and ended on the Simpasture playing fields. The festivities lasted two weeks overall.

Figure 97 – A Typical Scene from the Carnival Parade. Floats passing up Shafto Way

Chapter Eight

The 1980s

Following the growth in jobs and the new building of the 1970s, the 1980s quickly began to set a more depressed tone. In the 11th January 1980 edition of the Newton News the headline was that Eaton's factory had announced job losses and the tone for the decade was set. Apparently an order had been diverted to their Spanish affiliate because of ongoing industrial action at the Aycliffe factory. The estimate was that 200 jobs would be lost. It took until March of 1982 for an agreement between staff and owners to settle the dispute. By this time the factory had laid off hundreds of workers and was operating at 45% of its original size.

After taking over the housing stock from Aycliffe Development Corporation in 1978 Sedgefield District Council almost immediately began to try and deconstruct the original New Town concept of Newton Aycliffe. In January 1980 they proposed that all the green spaces in the older part of the new town should have older peoples' housing built on them. This did eventually occur at Gilpin Court. Harry Bilton was a determined advocate against this move pointing out that the Council controlled a lot of peripheral raw land (enough for a population of 45,000 people) and only had a population of 27,000 currently. There was no need for infill housing. To add to residents' misery the Sedgefield District Council announced rent, rates and water rate increases in April 1980.

In early 1981 rents were still increasing in the Town Centre and shops continued to close. Even the Town Council decided to move from the Town Centre into premises they bought from Rediffusion (the local provider of cable T.V. and radio) for £57,000. They moved in August of 1981 into their new premises on the outskirts of School Aycliffe near the entrance to The Oakleaf Centre. They cited inadequate space and high rents as the reasons for the move.

In May/June 1981 a new road was opened as an extension to Burnhill Way to link Newton Aycliffe to the newly proposed development at Woodham. The road cost £500,000.

Aycliffe Community Radio began to have problems and on the 1st June 1981 appointed Michael Searle as their new manager. He was quickly dismissed for unspecified issues and then reinstated in September 1981 but at 5:00pm on Tuesday the 12th January 1982 the station ceased broadcasting.

In August 1981 the Gretna Green Wedding Inn (as the 'Inn Cognito') changed hands again and reopened as 'Beejays' with a mixed 'disco' and bar motif.

On October 24th 1981, a service was held to celebrate the retirement of Major Elizabeth 'Bessie' Lincoln from the Salvation Army. Bessie was a familiar figure to all town residents either on her bike or walking and always visiting the pubs and clubs with a collection bucket.

The region also lost its 'Development Area' status and redundancies increased. By 1986 the total number of Trading Estate employees had dropped to less than 8000 from a peak over 10,000. Interestingly in the 1980s Newton Aycliffe and Peterlee provided two thirds of the total jobs coming into County Durham with the majority actually being in Peterlee.

The Town Centre also began to present further problems. In 1984 the Thames Centre (Figure 98) opened to a lukewarm reception – it had replaced the large, much-loved flower filled roundabout on St. Cuthbert's Way. In addition the Aycliffe Development Corporation sold the town centre to private ownership (The Grainger Trust).

More shops in the Town Centre began to close down and many were family shops that had been on the town since the early days (Hackett and Baines – moved to Darlington, The Wool Shop, Wentons). This type of closure was common across the region as unemployment increased, disposable income reduced, the trend to larger shops on 'out-of-town' sites was emerging. The situation had not been helped by the addition of shop sites 'up the ramp' and under it that felt dark and enclosed. The Town Centre had been expanded by making it oppressively compact.

The local press also began to negatively report Newton Aycliffe with campaigns to close Greenfield School in 1982 and 1986 as well as attempts to further rationalise school usage by bussing students from nearby Shildon.

Figure 98 - The Thames Centre (Photo from The Northern Echo)

When one shop closed it reported that most of its trade had come from residents with Department of Health and Social Security cheques and the press labelled Newton Aycliffe as 'Giro City'. The town was also found to have the highest incidence of solvent abuse, alcohol abuse and marital breakdown in the area. These were all symptoms of a rapid social decline and the population of Newton Aycliffe declined to 25,000.

In November 1981 the Aycliffe and Peterlee Development Corporations merged with the intention of creating some efficiencies in their latter years of existence. About 50 staff were made redundant to add to the unemployment and recession woes of the County in late 1981.

On a slightly more uplifting note, the Woodham Burn Nature Trail opened in late 1981 and the District Council set out its plans for the northern portion of Newton Aycliffe (basically the Woodham Development). The plan included the golf course, an equestrian centre, a small shopping precinct, a pub, even a hotel and a lot of private housing. They also took the opportunity to reduce their estimate of the Town's population further from 34,000 to 32,000.

Aycliffe Development Corporation eventually sold the Trading Estate to a company called Helical Bar in 1987 and being at the end of its mandate the Aycliffe Development Corporation was dissolved on the 1st December 1988 after 40 years of effort.

The central Government was heavily encouraging local authorities to begin selling off social housing to sitting tenants in the 1980s. This presented Great Aycliffe Town Council with a problem – much of their older housing stock had been built as inexpensively as possible and some houses were found to be unsafe. The original ORLIT/UNITY built homes were declared unsafe after a series of inspections – as described earlier this was due to ongoing rusting and expansion of the reinforcing steel. This produced fractures in the concrete support structure. Unfortunately many people had purchased these homes under the scheme whereby residents of council housing stock could purchase the homes at advantageous prices. The council offered to buy the houses back at then prevailing market prices. Many of these houses were then demolished (see earlier example photo from Shafto Way).

The first generation of ORLIT/UNITY houses in the Clarence Chare area were found to be not subject to long-term corrosion and were subsequently declared safe. The former owners then banked the capital gain from the sale back to the council and became council tenants again. These houses remain in the older part of town with many having been re-surfaced with brick and render.

Figure 99 - Left ORLIT/UNITY built home as originally built

Same home shown in 2018

On January 9th 1980 Dr. David Bellamy opened 'The Turbinia' pub in the Parson's Centre on Sid Chaplin Way, another sign of the town's ongoing expansion to the northwest.

The approval in February 1980 of the private development of Woodham Village was perhaps the most positive event of the 1980s. Construction began in 1981 with a very ambitious program to build 1000 houses, the centre with shops, a pub, a church, the golf course and the equestrian centre.

In early 1982 The Sunday Times, in a study of schools, described Newton Aycliffe as 'a drab, post-war new town' and its children as 'a lively but rather bored breed in humdrum Newton Aycliffe'. Not a glowing testimony!

The Aycliffe Development Corporation took over land on the south side of the Industrial Estate in 1982 that included the old Stock Car Stadium. This was to be used to build more factories. As mentioned earlier the Stock Car Stadium lasted until 1989 before final removal.

The late 1980s and into the 1990s saw a general upswing in the economy. This rejuvenated industry in Newton Aycliffe, with Flymo and Talents both announcing expansions in 1988. In 1989 Hydro Polymers (formerly Bakelite, BXL and Perstorp) announced a £50 million extension and 3M intended to invest £10 million.

Chapter Nine

The 1990s

Industrial investment continued to boost the general economy as well as the local Newton Aycliffe one. By the end of 1994 Sanyo and Fujitsu invested heavily with Fujitsu alone investing £300 million in its factory.

The removal of older infrastructure continued and in 1992 The Avenue Comprehensive School (formerly Marlowe and Milton Hall Schools) was demolished and in 1993 / 1994 Aycliffe Hospital was closed.

The Town Centre was still a contentious issue in early 1995 with a headline article in the Newton News demanding that the owners seek to attract new businesses and make it a viable shopping area. The Town Centre had been sold on to the Freshwater Group who were London-based and regarded as 'absentee landlords' with little interest in local shoppers welfare.

In mid March 1995 the new leader of the Labour Party and future Prime Minister Tony Blair visited Newton Aycliffe as part of his Sedgefield constituency. Over 300 people crammed into the Sycamore Suite at the Newton Aycliffe Leisure Centre to hear him speak and he presented former mayor Win Dormer with a special merit award for her 25 years of service as Labour Group secretary. In mid April 1995, prior to the May local elections, it was announced that Labour had already taken a majority on the Great Aycliffe Town Council before any votes were cast because so many of their candidates ran unopposed.

Newton Aycliffe was designated to be part of the 50th anniversary celebration of V.E. Day (Victory in Europe Day). This was to involve the erection of a fire basket on the hill overlooking the Oakleaf playing fields as part of a national beacon chain. The event occurred on Monday the 8th May 1995 at 8:40pm and was lit by the mayor Cllr. Peter Gowton. The beacon was lit a second time on the 15th August to celebrate V.J. Day (Victory over Japan Day and end of WW2).

The Newton News of June 10th 1995 contains a letter from Vera Chapman appealing for photos for her book 'Around Newton Aycliffe' which was due to be assembled (Chapman, 1995).

On July 16th 1995, St. Clare's Church celebrated the 40th anniversary of its original opening. Special guests were Cynthia Hugill and Eric Batchelor (Mr and Mrs Batchelor) who were the first couple to be married in the facility in 1955.

At the end of July 1995, Sedgefield District Council produced its preliminary plan for the ongoing development of the Aycliffe Industrial Park. A group made up of representatives of several interested parties collaborated to produce the plan. At the core of the plan was the redevelopment of older sites within the Park as well as better general landscaping, better entrances and exits and better roads through the Park.

Figure 100 – Aycliffe Nature Park – formally 'The Newt Ponds' on the site of Demon's Bridge railway station serving the munitions factory from World War 2. (Photo courtesy of 'The Newton News')

Aycliffe Nature Park won the Northumbrian Britain in Bloom award for Best Conservation Project in 1995 – the Park was a redevelopment of the area probably known to many as 'the newt ponds' (formally the site of Demon's Bridge railway station during WW2) and was the result of much volunteer work led by the group's chairman Ben Hardaker.

The Sanyo factory in Newton Aycliffe celebrated the production of its one-millionth microwave oven in 1995.

Having demolished The Avenue Comprehensive School the various branches of government began to contemplate the future of the site and meetings were held beginning in 1995. From contemporary reports it seems that the area was always going to be used to begin to 'fix' the poorly designed existing town centre.

On the 19th August 1995, local dentist Mr. C.H. Stafford retired after 41 years of service to the town. He occupied premises at 17, Finchale Road (above Dr. Parker's surgery) for many years before moving to purpose-built premises at Simpasture.

On September 16th, Newton Aycliffe's first large grocery store was set to close. Walter Willsons at the Town Centre cited out of town superstore competition and high Town Centre rents as the cause of closure.

The Gretna Green Wedding Inn continued its evolution, announcing the building of an 18-room motel on the back of the existing hotel on the 18th November 1995. In September 1996 the Gretna re-opened after its £2.5 million renovation under the ownership of the Big Steak pub chain.

In early December 1995 a second attempt at a local radio station occurred. A1 FM 103.2 was a channel specifically for Darlington and Newton Aycliffe. The schedule was published weekly in the Newton News. By the end of the year this was recast as Alpha FM 103.2 and designed to cover Darlington, Newton Aycliffe and Sedgefield.

The summer of 1996 seems to have been characterised in 'The Newton News' by many articles and letters related to the sad state of the Town Centre – the only highlight being the re-opening of a town favourite - F.W. Woolworths after renovation. At the end of October 1996, Somerfield/Gateway opened in the premises formerly occupied by Finefare maintaining the presence of a larger supermarket on the town.

On October 24th 1996, Sedgefield District achieved Borough status, the only effect of which appears to be that it got a Mayor!

In early November 1996 there was an impromptu visit to Newton Aycliffe by Andrew, the Duke of York. He spent 2.5 hours at Aycliffe Young People's Centre that had benefitted from his patronage for the previous ten years.

As mentioned earlier, 1996 saw the mysterious disappearance of the ceremonial spade and turf-box associated with the original sod cutting ceremony as the New Town was formed. The Chief Officer of the Town Council, John Farquhar, had been Chief Officer for 28 years and was dismissed for additional 'gross misconduct' after a five and a half hour hearing. The nature of the 'misconduct' was related to financial malfeasance, but suspicions were also voiced that he was associated with the missing spade and box.

In October 1997, 'The Newton News' described the missing spade and asked Mr. Farquhar if he knew where it was. He said the last time he saw it was in the Council chambers. Mr. Farquhar passed away in 2005 and in 2009, in an unrelated criminal investigation at his former home in Houghton-Le-Side the spade and box were recovered from the attic.

In 1997 the sitting Member of Parliament for the Sedgefield constituency (which includes Newton Aycliffe) became the Prime Minister – Tony Blair. This brought the area to the nation's attention with foreign dignitaries visiting the constituency including French President Jacques Chirac and US President George W. Bush.

Hydro Polymers Ltd. opened their new £35 million expansion on their site (formally Bakelite, BXL and Perstorp) in time to celebrate the 50th year of PVC manufacture on that site.

In September 1997 it was announced that Aycliffe Hospital would be demolished to make way for a housing development. Despite there being minor dissent at Council level this planning permission passed relatively smoothly.

The Sedgefield Borough Council began to introduce systems into Newton Aycliffe to enrich the lives of the aging residents. These included an alert system for older people (Carelink) at a cost of £1 million, the 'Community Force' and in 1998 a Carers Centre (The Pioneering Care Centre at Cobbler's Hall – the foundation stone was laid by Tony Blair on the 6th November 1998). In addition an Early Learning Centre and an Environmental Ranger were put in place for younger residents.

The fiftieth anniversary of Newton Aycliffe was celebrated in 1998 and revitalised some civic pride. As 1998 began it was clear that the 50th anniversary was going to be a big event. Initial plans involved the Rotary Club and targeted June 20th to 28th. The Prime Minister (Tony Blair) was expected to attend (if available) as well as local Mayors. Sadly Tony Blair failed to attend any of the anniversary events much to the chagrin of local councillors.

Events were planned to begin with a fair and exhibition at the Leisure Centre showcasing the town's contribution to local industry and ending with a multi-denominational church service. The Town Council focused its fiftieth anniversary celebration on the establishment of The Great Aycliffe Way – a continuous circular footpath around the boundary of the town. The preparation for the path began when the first 'sod' was cut in early August 1997 by the Mayors of Sedgefield Borough and Great Aycliffe (Brian Avery and Sarah Iveson respectively). This footpath is much valued by residents and links a number of nature areas and incorporates the disused Clarence Railway track bed.

During the 1990s residents appear to have ceased to complain about the lack of facilities and begun to focus on ''smaller' problems such as 'wheelie bins', dog fouling and bad neighbours. This recognised that residents had now become used to Newton Aycliffe as 'home' without it having to be all things to all residents. People were prepared to travel to nearby towns for elements of their recreation without having them built on the town itself. Persistent 'bigger' issues in Newton Aycliffe continued to be crime (mostly theft / break-ins – up to 100 a month around Christmas time in 1995), vandalism, drug use, teenage homelessness and the state of the Town Centre throughout the 1990s (including the long delay in planning and building on the former Avenue Comprehensive site). The Newton News of the 1990s seems to be characterised by an endless stream of letters from Town Councillors in a series of 'disagreements' with each other.

Chapter Ten

Post Millennial Newton Aycliffe

Figure 101 - Newton Aycliffe iconic clock tower in 2018 – Thames Centre in the background, Churchill House demolished. All part of Phase 4 of the Regeneration Masterplan. Photo - Robin Hornsby

There is a strong sense of rejuvenation associated with the modern Newton Aycliffe. Older infrastructure is being removed and replaced with new. The addition of broad swathes of new, privately owned homes on the north bank of Woodham Burn, has increased the population to approximately 26,600. The Town Centre has / is undergoing a complete renovation with Churchill House being demolished (The iconic 77 foot clock tower has been preserved!).

The addition of a large Tesco Superstore on the site of The Avenue Comprehensive School in 2003 / 2004 now attracts modern, motorised shoppers to the town.

In early February 2005, a pioneer shopkeeper, Harry Harding, passed away. He had run the much-loved Harding's Toy Shop in the Town Centre for many years. Harding's was the first shop to open in the Town Centre before it relocated to 'up the ramp'.

As a result of continued inaction on revitalising the Town Centre and allowing the Health Centre to more or less collapse, the election of 2007 returned a 'hung' Town Council with 50% opposition councillors and 50% Labour. This was only the second time the Council was not Labour dominated.

Figure 102 – The infamous ramp in the central Town Centre – The photo dates from Christmas 2008, since Woolworths is having a 'closing down' sale that happened on 2nd January 2009 (Photo courtesy of 'The Newton News')

In 2007 the owners of the Town Centre shopping area (now Daejan Durham Ltd) formed an informal partnership with Great Aycliffe Town Council; Sedgefield Borough Council; Durham County Council; County Durham PCT; and Tees Esk and Wear Valley NHS Trust. The purpose of this association was to develop a forward plan for the Town Centre. In 2008 a plan was eventually put in place to deal with the town centre problem. It consisted of multiple phases a number of which were already accomplished by 2013.

Phases 1 through 3 were complete, or in progress, and consisted of reconfiguring the Somerfield store, relocating the Health Centre (it was split to the Cobblers Hall area and into The Thames Centre), demolishing Dalton Way and building the Aldi retail development. This latter was completed by November 2012 and included a link to Tesco.

The Library was temporarily moved to the site of the former Central Avenue service station. Phase 3 was underway in 2013, and included improvements to the public area (shop fronts, canopies etc.) as well as the removal of ramps and stairways. Later phases would relocate Durham County Council services into the leisure centre, as well as demolish and rebuild some older retail blocks.

In 2008 Woodham Technology College Sixth Form was closed which was taken as a major status blow for the town.

Figure 103 – The sculpture "In Our Own Image" by Joseph Hillier – It stands at the southern entrance to the Aycliffe Business Park. (Photo taken by Tony Griffiths and provided courtesy of Aycliffe Fabrications).

Towards the end of January 2009, the art installation that currently stands at the southern entrance to the Aycliffe Business Park began to be created. Called 'In Our Image' (and informally called 'The Head'), it is a 16-metre tall steel framework in the shape of a head with the outlines of several workers placed on it. The artist was Joseph Hillier and the structure was built by Aycliffe Fabrications.

Sedgefield Borough Council was abolished in 2009 and Newton Aycliffe was absorbed into the Durham County Council unitary authority. Shortly after this, all the social housing and land previously held by the Borough Council was handed over to a 'social landlord' - Sedgefield Borough Homes. This came with its fair share of controversy - accusations that Sedgefield Borough Homes was made up of former councillors who would pay nothing for the 8000+ homes plus associated land. Many complaints were voiced in 'The Newton News', the commonest probably being the intent of Sedgefield Borough Homes to build on grass areas, particularly in the newer parts of the town.

Apparently only renting tenants were allowed to participate in any votes, which left homeowners feeling disenfranchised, particularly in areas of mostly home ownership.

In December 2009 a new 1200-seat conference facility – the Xcel Centre – opened on Aycliffe Business Park.

On 6th November 2010, the Industrial Estate again demonstrated the ongoing dangers associated with manufacturing. The Stillers Storage facility, containing stored aerosols caught fire and burned for several days, sending a large smoke cloud across South Durham.

The former Southerne Club at Hawkshead Place was demolished in 2012 after standing empty for a number of years.

In September 2013 Durham County Council issued 'The Newton Aycliffe Regeneration Masterplan' which attempts to summarise the regeneration and investment strategy that is in progress or planned. In this document the Durham County Council makes a number of commitments to assist Newton Aycliffe in its evolution. Specifically they will support the Aycliffe Business Park and company expansion with a goal to double the number of jobs in the supply chain related to the Hitachi Rail development. Secondly they will work with the private sector to deliver successful and sustainable housing expansion. Thirdly they will work with partners to continue to deliver the Aycliffe Shopping Centre Masterplan. These all seem to strike at the heart of modern needs for residents of Newton Aycliffe - jobs, housing and fixing the long term Town Centre problem. It is anticipated that this will cost £16 million in public investment and attract £224 million in private investment over the next 30 years.

Statistically, Newton Aycliffe and Middridge had a combined population of 26,300 that had seen a rise in the 85+ age group and a fall in the 5 to 15 age group in 2012. There was a working population of 16,693.

In 2015 the Aycliffe Festival replaced the Great Aycliffe Show as the centrepiece of summer revelry in Newton Aycliffe - the change was from a single site 'showground' with many events hosted, to smaller events dispersed around the town.

Newton Aycliffe has attained regional significance in the art world by hosting significant exhibitions at the Greenfield Gallery (co-sited with Greenfield College). Currently (2019) an exhibition by famed north eastern social artist, Norman Cornish, is on display, reflecting life in the coal mining villages whose closure provided so many to the work force that migrated to Newton Aycliffe.

Always at the core of Newton Aycliffe's being has been the jobs provided by the Trading Estate. The factories on the Trading Estate are now a modern suite of buildings with almost all of the original ROF 59 buildings gone. The most recent coup has been based on almost the same criteria as that which governed the selection of the site for ROF 59. The Hitachi Rail Factory commenced building in 2013 and was officially opened on 3rd September 2015, in the presence of Hiroaki Nakanishi (Hitachi); Patrick McLoughlin (MP); Claire Perry (MP); George Osborne (MP); David Cameron (Prime Minister of the United Kingdom); and 500 guests.

It initially created 420 jobs, and aims to employ more than 700 people at maximum capacity. Hitachi were able to leverage the availability of large industrial sites; the proximity of rail and road links; and a local, skilled labour force. The factory was built at Merchant Park, owned by Merchant Park Development, and took up 32 acres of a 70-acre site. Prior to construction, Wardell Armstrong LLP undertook an archaeological excavation and, as mentioned earlier, evidence of Iron Age roundhouses was found.

On the 29th October 2018, a sad event occurred - the passing of Syd Howarth who was the long-time editor of 'The Newton News', the town news magazine that continued on from 'The Newtonian' established in 1950. Syd was often referred to as 'Mr. Newton Aycliffe' and had published the magazine since 1963.

There is recognition in the Masterplan that Newton Aycliffe is no longer an insular society with workers living adjacent to their factories and their needs serviced exclusively by shops and recreation opportunities in Newton Aycliffe. Modern society is significantly more mobile, working over a broad area, shopping throughout the county and driving to recreation wherever it may be.

So a town that began as an enormous social 'experiment' (an icon of that genre in fact!) had eventually returned to a dominantly private sector enterprise.

What does the future hold? Newton Aycliffe is continuing to grow, with housing applications in for 950 new houses on the east side of the Great North Road for the first time at Low Copelaw (See Figure 105). These are proposed to be in the area of the Aycliffe Secure Centre.

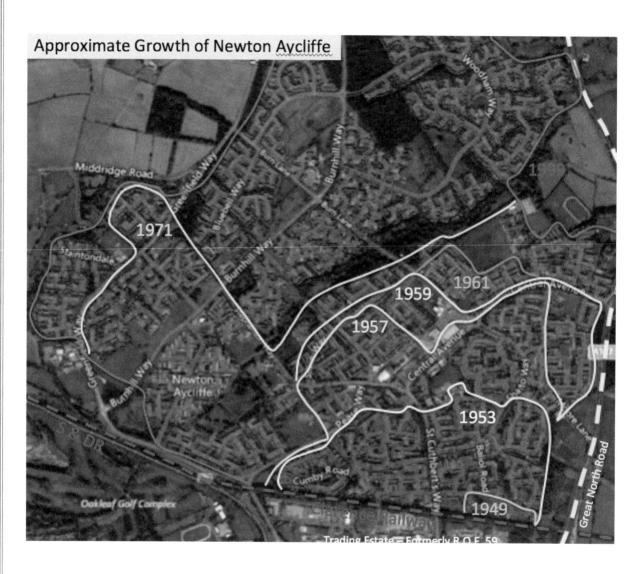

Figure 104 - An Attempt to visually represent the various extents of Newton Aycliffe during its growth based on the 'Tenants Handbook' maps and projected on a modern satellite image.

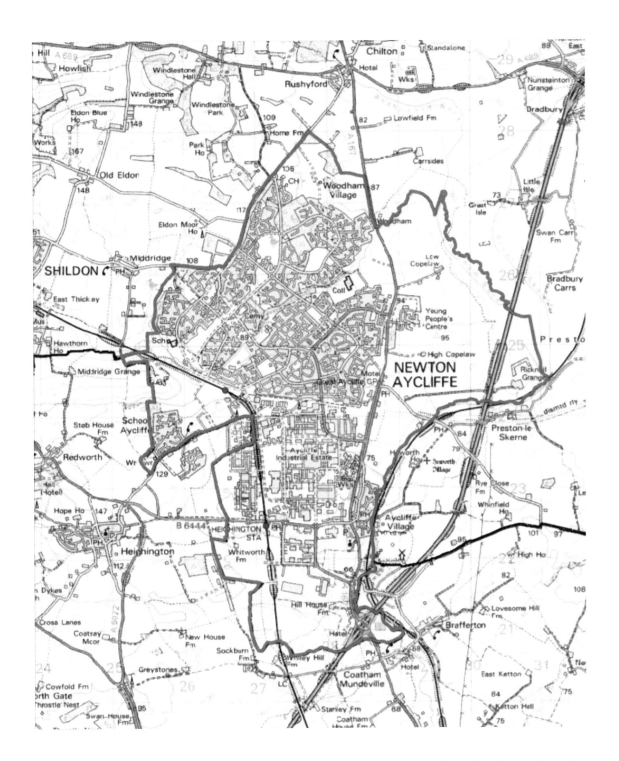

Figure 105 – The current vision of Newton Aycliffe's future growth shown by the red outline (Taken with permission from The Great Aycliffe Town Council – Great Aycliffe Neighbourhood Plan, 2017)

References/Bibliography

Aberdeen, Stella (1968) A File of personal recollections held at Newton Aycliffe Library and covering 1948 – 1968.

Aberdeen, Stella (1970) Newton Aycliffe – The Beginning of a New Town. Correspondence in the Durham County Local History Society.

Aycliffe Village Local History Group website – contains a number of Newton Aycliffe photos, a wealth of data on the Great Aycliffe parish. http://www.aycliffehistory.org.uk/html/newtonaycliffe.html

Beveridge, Lord William (1949) Summary of Report Accompanying Plan of Aycliffe New Town with Preface (N0 31) Copy held by Durham Record Centre, Ref. No. NT/AP 1/5/38.

Beveridge, Lord William: Archive files held at the London School of Economics Library. File Nos. BEV /7/28, BEV /7/19, BEV /7/20, BEV /7/21.

The Beveridge Papers from the British Library of Political and Economic Science Part 3: Correspondence and Papers on Health Services, Old Age, Pensions, New Towns and Post War Europe, 1919 - 1962 On Microfilm, Reel 57.

Bowden, Peter (1978) The Origins of Newton Aycliffe, In: Mining and Social Change – Durham County in the Twentieth Century. Editor: Martin Bulmer, Published by Croom Helm Ltd, and Reprinted in 2015 by Routledge.

Boyes, David (2007) An exercise in gracious living: the northeast new towns 1947-1988, Durham theses, Durham University. Available at Durham E-Theses Online: http://etheses.dur.ac.uk/2335/

Chandran, Arun M. (2018) Website maintained by a former deputy leader of Great Aycliffe Town Council. http://www.greataycliffe.com/id24.html

Chapman, Vera (1995) Around Newton Aycliffe, The Archive Photographs Series, The Chalford Publishing Company, ISBN 0 7524 0327 3

Clare, John D. (2018) Town History – A page of history of Newton Aycliffe that appears on the Newton News website. This has been particularly useful for the period 1970 to present. http://www.newtonnews.co.uk/local-information/town-history/

Clare, John D. (2019) A Seven-Part Series on the History of Newton Aycliffe. Published in The Newton News, July – August 2019.

O'Connor, Gladys (2018) A Far Off Bell. Pub: Amazon, Edited by Philip Atkinson. ISBN 9781722770402

Cooper, Chris (2013) The Great North Road – Then and Now. Published by: After the Battle. ISBN 978-1870067799.

Darlington Rural District Council (1949) Annual Report for 1949, at: https://archive.org/stream/b29149708/b29149708_djvu.txt

Durham County Council (2013) Newton Aycliffe Regeneration Masterplan, September 2013, Draft 4, Version 12 (Final, Cabinet) at www.democracy.durham.gov.uk

Edwards, Brian (1968) An interview with Lillian Holmes entitled 'The Town That Grew Out of the Mud'. The Newtonian, December 1968, Page 3.

Gittins, John (1952) Approved School Boys. Pub: London: Her Majesty's Stationery Office.

Great Aycliffe Coronation Souvenir Handbook (1953) (Copy held at Durham Records Centre, Ref. No. NT/AP 1/5/252).

The Great Aycliffe Town Council website which contains a large number of photographs of the New Town through time. http://www.great-aycliffe.gov.uk/about/historic-picture-gallery/

Great Aycliffe Town Council (2017) Information for Mayor, Appendix C – A Brief History of Great Aycliffe – likely authored by John D. Clare.

Great Aycliffe Town Council (2017) Neighbourhood Plan, Version 4, Referendum, June 2017.

Grenfell Baines Group (1948) Newton Aycliffe: Original Master Plan Report on the Development of the Designated Area (No. 100), December 1948. (Copy held at Durham Records Centre, Ref. No. NT/AP 1/5/94.

Grenfell Baines Group (1949) Newton Aycliffe Master Plan (No. 110), approximately 1949. (Copy held at Durham Records Centre, Ref. No. NT/AP 1/5/102).

Hailsham (1963) The North East: A Program For Change (The Hailsham Report), November 1963.

Newton Aycliffe Regeneration Master Plan (2013) Durham County Council, Draft 4, Version 12, September 2013.

Newton Aycliffe (1969) Article in the Durham County Local History Society.

Newton Aycliffe 'Tenants Handbook' (1953) The Aycliffe Development Corporation. (Personal Copy)

Newton Aycliffe 'Tenants Handbook' (1955) The Aycliffe Development Corporation. (Personal Copy)

Newton Aycliffe 'Tenants Handbook' (1957) The Aycliffe Development Corporation. (Personal Copy)

Newton Aycliffe 'Tenants Handbook' (1959) The Aycliffe Development Corporation. (Personal Copy)

Newton Aycliffe 'Tenants Handbook' (1961) The Aycliffe Development Corporation. (Personal Copy)

Newton Aycliffe 'Tenants Handbook' (1964) The Aycliffe Development Corporation. (Copy held at Durham Records Office, Ref. No. NT/AP 1/5/42)

Newton Aycliffe 'Tenants Handbook' (1969) The Aycliffe Development Corporation. (Copy held at Durham Records Office, Ref. No. NT/AP 1/5/130)

Newton Aycliffe 'Tenants Handbook' (1973) The Aycliffe Development Corporation. (Copy held at Durham Records Office, Ref. No. NT/AP 1/5/39)

Newton Aycliffe Town Guide Anniversary Souvenir Edition (1998/1999), Printed by The Newton Press in conjunction with Great Aycliffe Town Council.

'The Newton News' website which contains an archive of back issues of its precursor 'The Newtonian' from 1958 as well as a file of old photographs and a short history of Newton Aycliffe, written at least in part by John D. Clare. http://www.newtonnews. co.uk/local-information/town-history/

The Parish Church of St. Clare, Newton Aycliffe (1980). 25th Anniversary Silver Jubilee Souvenir.

Philipson, Garry (1988) Aycliffe and Peterlee New Towns 1946 – 1988 Swords into Ploughshares and Farewell Squalor. Pub: Publications for Companies. ISBN 09049282117.

Reports of the Development Corporations for the period ended 31st March 1967. Pub: London: Her Majesty's Stationery Office.

The Windlestone Estate Sale Documents (1936): Catalog of Properties for Auction held on 12th November 1936 at the Kings Head Hotel, Darlington. (Copy held at Historic England Archive, Swindon, Catalogue No. 1585 / EST 01 / Ref. SC00325)

This is The North-East – ROF 59 website sponsored by Northumbria University - http://www.communigate.co.uk/ne/aycliffeangels/index.phtml

Appendix One

Physical Descriptions of Farmhouses, Cottages etc. from the Newton Aycliffe Area (Transcribed from the Windlestone Estate Sale documents of 1936). The majority of these buildings were demolished to make way for either modification to the Great North Road, the construction of ROF 59 or for the construction of Newton Aycliffe itself. Their names live on in many cases as the names of areas, buildings or roads in the new town. If the name of a property is shown in red the property still exists today (2018). Only building descriptions are listed here, farmland offerings have been omitted. Lot numbers are shown on the index map in Figure 106. In addition at the end of this appendix are some photos of farms or cottages that weren't in the sale (because they weren't owned by the Eden Estate) but are included here for completeness.

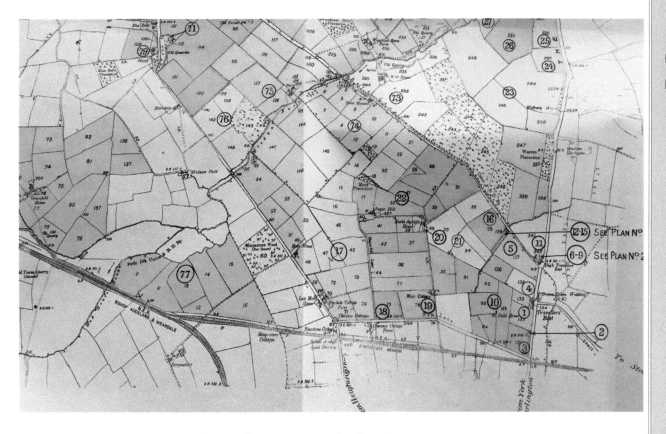

Figure 106 - Index map for the Windlestone Estate Sale of 1936.

Lot 1 – The buildings associated with The Travellers' Rest (formerly the Bay Horse public house).

A Valuable Small Holding extending to about 5 acres, 2 roods and 11 poles. Formerly the 'Bay Horse' Inn.

Situated on the Great North Road, to which it has about 550ft of frontage.

The House – is stone built and cement faced, with pantiled roof, and contains three bedrooms, sitting room, kitchen, scullery and dairy.

The Buildings – mostly stone built with tiled roofs, comprise cow house for 11; brick and tiled calf house for 2 and pen; loose box, cow house for 10. Being Ordnance Nos. 133, 134 and 138 in Great Aycliffe Parish and let to Mr. Robert Walton with other lands on a yearly (13th May) tenancy. Apportioned rent £15 10s 0d per annum.

Apportioned Outgoings: Tithe (commuted): 7s 8d.

Figure 107 - View north along the Great North Road showing The Travellers' Rest on the left (Lot 1 in the sale), The Gretna Green Wedding Inn (not in the sale) on the right and four cottages of High Travellers' Rest in the distance (Lots 6, 7, 8, 9).

Lot 2 – (a small cottage on the Great North Road, between the Travellers' Rest and the Clarence Railway). A detached cottage, stone built with tiled roof, containing a bedroom, kitchen, back kitchen and small garden, coal house etc., in all about 18 poles being part of Ord. No. 139 in Great Aycliffe Parish. Let to Mr. Robert Palmer on a weekly tenancy at £7 16s 0d per annum.

Lot 6 – A Cottage at High Travellers' Rest, being one of a terrace of four occupying an important position at the corner of the Great North Road and Burn Lane. It is stone built, with pantiled roof and brick chimneys and contains two bedrooms, kitchen and back kitchen, together with stable, wash-house and garden, in all about 22 poles. Being part of Ord. No. 342 in Woodham Parish. Let to Mr. Greatorex on a weekly tenancy at £14 6s. 0d. Per annum. Landlord paying rates. The terrace was demolished during the 1950s / Early 1960s – local residents remember it as well as the ruins after demolition. Keith Mews recalls the stone from those houses being taken to build a bungalow on Burn Lane near Woodham Burn.

Figure 108 - High Travellers' Rest Cottages (Lots 6, 7, 8, 9). Shown in the late 1950s/early 1960s. (From Chapman, 1995)

Lot 7 – The adjoining cottage of similar construction and containing two bedrooms, living kitchen, divided into two, and garden, extending in all to about 9 poles being part of Ordnance No. 342 in Woodham Parish and let to Mr. John Watson on a weekly tenancy at £13 per annum. Landlord paying rates.

Lot 8 - The adjoining cottage of similar construction and containing two bedrooms, kitchen, back kitchen, in all about 4 poles being part of Ordnance No. 342 in Woodham Parish and let to Mrs. R. Wake on a weekly tenancy at £13 per annum. Landlord paying rates.

Lot 9 – The adjoining and similar cottage with good garden, extending to about 14 poles being part of Ord. No. 342 in Woodham Parish and let to Mr. E. Pratt on a weekly tenancy at £15 12s. 0d. per annum. Landlord paying rates. A right as at present enjoyed to a supply of water from a well and pump included in this lot is reserved in favour of Lots 6, 7 and 8 subject to payment of a proportionate part of the cost of upkeep.

Lot 12 – A cottage being one of four known as 'Tannery Cottages' (also known as Tanyard Cottages) situated in Burn Lane. Stone built with slated roof and brick chimneys and containing two bedrooms, kitchen, scullery and garden extending to about 1 rood being part of Ordnance Nos. 128 and 129 in Great Aycliffe Parish. Let to Mr. W.J.W. Hunter on a weekly tenancy at £13 17s. 4d. per annum. Landlord paying rates.

Lot 13 – The adjoining and similar cottage extending with good garden and range of old stone, brick and tiled buildings to about 32 poles. Being part of Ordnance Nos. 128 and 129 in Great Aycliffe Parish. Let to Mrs. Everson on a weekly tenancy at £6 18s. 8d. per annum. Landlord paying rates. The right as at present enjoyed to a supply of water from the well and pump included with this lot is reserved in favour of lots 12, 14 and 15.

Figure 109 - Grainy magnified air photo showing older buildings on Burn/Moore Lane prior to demolition – Photo likely from early 1954 courtesy Great Aycliffe Town Council.

Figure 110 - A young Desnee Charlton in front of the only known picture of Tannery Cottages (also known as 'Tanyard Cottages') – Photo from Desnee Charlton via Facebook

Lot 14 - The adjoining and similar cottage extending with good garden and range of old stone, brick and tiled buildings to about 33 poles. Being part of Ordnance Nos. 128 and 129 in Great Aycliffe Parish. Let to Mrs. T. Birbeck on a weekly tenancy at £13 17s. 4d. per annum. Landlord paying rates.

Lot 15 - The adjoining and similar cottage extending to about 4 poles. Being part of Ordnance Nos. 128 in Great Aycliffe Parish. Let to Mrs. Wardle on a weekly tenancy at £6 1s. 4d. per annum. Landlord paying rates.

Lot 17 – An important mixed farm known as Finchale Cottage Farm having long road frontages and extending to about 100 acres, 0 roods, and 12 poles. The house is stone built and tiled and creeper covered, contains five bedrooms, two sitting rooms, kitchen, back kitchen, dairy. Water from well and pump. The farm buildings comprise modern three bay cart shed, two brick and slate loose boxes, smithy, stone and tiled cow house for 5, stable for 3 and loft, cart horse stabling for 3 and loft, stone and tiled barn and granary, calf house, cow house for 8, piggery. There are off-buildings known as Moor House comprising two old stone and tiled loose boxes, implement shed, small yard and two bay cattle shed. Mr. R.S. Crusher and Mr. William Clement share tenancy of the associated land.

Figure 111 - Finchale Cottage Farm, Lot 17 (From Chapman, 1995)

Lot 19 – includes Moor Cottage that is stone built and pantiled, contains two bedrooms, kitchen, small room. Adjoining are two small cow byres. Water from well. Being Ordnance Nos. 35 and 78 in Great Aycliffe Parish. Let with other lands to Mr. William Clementon a yearly tenancy (13th May). Apportioned rent £19 per annum.

Lot 20 – An attractive residence known as North Aycliffe House, stone built with slated roof, containing five bedrooms, two sitting rooms, kitchen, back kitchen and pantry. The buildings comprise stone and slated coach house and stable, coalhouse, good brick and slated cow byre for 2 and a loose box. Extending with land, orchard and garden to about 1 acre, 3 roods and 11 poles. Being part of Ordnance Nos. 38 and pt. 39 in Great Aycliffe Parish. Partially let to R.S. Crusher (£1 per annum) and part to Mr. T. Boddington (£19 10s. 0d. per annum)

Lot 22 – An attractive medium sized farm known as Sugar Hill Farm having frontages to Burn Lane and Sugar Hill Lane extending to about 58 acres, 3 roods and 31 poles. The house is stone built and cement faced, and contains four bedrooms, sitting room, kitchen, back kitchen, pantry, milk house. Water from well and pump. The farm buildings are mostly stone built and tiled, comprise a wheel shed, cow house for 8, two bay wood cart shed, four stalled cow byre, calf pen, piggery, calf house for 6, implement shed and granary, two brick boarded and tiled loose boxes. Let with other lands to Mr. R.S. Crusher on a yearly tenancy (13th May). Apportioned rent £105 per annum.

Lot 23 – An important holding known as Welbury House Farm having nearly 2000 ft. of valuable frontage to the Great North Road, extending to about 96 acres, 2 roods, 29 poles. The house is brick built and slated contains 3 bedrooms, kitchen, back kitchen, washhouse, dairy, coalhouse etc. Water from well by semi-rotary pump. The buildings comprise a brick and slate two-stall stable, two cow houses for 8 each, meal house. Mostly let to Mr. G.O. Charlton on a yearly tenancy (13th May) at £70 per annum.

Figure 112 – Welbury House Farm as it exists today (2018)

Lot 27 – A small holding being part of Woodham South Farm extending to about 10 acres, 1 rood, 6 poles. The small house is stone and brick built with tiled roof, contains four bedrooms, two sitting rooms, two kitchens, dairy, well of water. The buildings comprise cow house for 6, piggery, four-stalled stable and granary, two bay cart shed and barn, hay house, cow house for 12. Milk house, two bay yard, two-stalled stable and box, Rick yard. Being Ord. Nos. 252, 251, 249 and pt. 253 in Woodham Parish. Let to Mr. Robert Orton with other lands on a yearly (13th May) tenancy. Apportioned rent £18 per annum.

Lot 29 – The important farm known as Woodham Farm. Bounded on the East for its entire length by the Great North Road, extending to about 156 acres, 1 rood, 15 poles. The superior house is brick built and slated, contains five bedrooms, bathroom (with hot and cold), box room, drawing room, dining room, back kitchen. Water from estate supply. The farm buildings comprise three-bay timber cart shed, implement shed and granary, cow house for 13, barn and hay store, loose box, yard with cow byre for 10, another yard with cow byre for 8, six calf pens, stabling for 6. This lot is let to Messrs. J. Hopps and sons on a yearly tenancy (13th May) at £180 per annum including water.

Figure 113 - Woodham Farm – House and Outbuildings (Lot 29).

Lot 31 – The attractive detached residence known as Woodham House situated adjoining the Great North Road and extending with garden and paddock to about 1 acre, 1 rood, 7 poles. Brick built, rough cast with slated gabled roof, the house contains a drawing room, dining room, bar room, kitchen, dairy, back kitchen, pantry, W.C. and wash basin, cellars. On the first floor are bar with tap room at rear, drawing room, dining room and two other rooms now used as bedrooms. On the second floor are six bedrooms (four with fireplaces), bathroom, separate W.C., box room. Water from estate supply. Brick built and tiled stabling and garage. Being part of Ord. Nos. 262 and 262a in Woodham Parish. Let to Mr. Robert Bowes on a yearly tenancy (13th May) at £30 per annum (including water).

The description of this lot suggests that it used to be 'The Rising Stag' public house associated with the Great North Road.

Figure 114 - Woodham House, formerly 'The Rising Stag Inn' (gabled building to the left) with two adjoining semi-detached cottages to the right. In all Lots 31, 32, 33.

Lot 32 – An attractive semi-detached cottage brick built, roughcast and slated. Containing three bedrooms, kitchen, back kitchen, pantry with sink. Water from estate supply, extending to about 7 poles. Being part of Ord. No. 262a in Woodham Parish and let to Mr. J. Wallis on a quarterly tenancy at £8 per annum (including water). The yard running at the back of this and Lot 33 is used jointly by the owners and occupiers of these lots and shall continue to be so used.

Lot 33 – The adjoining and similar cottage extending to about 5 poles. Being part of Ord. No. 262a in Woodham Parish and let to Mr. J. Dodsworth on a weekly tenancy at £8 0s. 4d. per annum (including water).

Lot 70 – An important stock and mixed farm known as Cobblers Hall Farm occupying an important position at the junction of Middridge Lane, Burn Lane and another good parish road, extending in all to about 185 acres, 3 roods, 29 poles. The house is stone built, cement faced, brick chimneys with tiled gabled roof, contains three bedrooms, sitting room, kitchen and back kitchen. Water from well and pump. Garden. The farm buildings comprise cart-horse stabling for 4, cow house for 8 with feeding passage, ditto for 4, two calf pens, cow house for 6 with feeding passage. Piggery, two loose boxes, dairy, two cart sheds, cow house for 5 or 6, meal house, two implement sheds, small yard and cattle shed. The plantations Ord. Nos. 96 and 189 are in hand and the remainder is let to Mr. Reginald Dent on a yearly tenancy (13th May) at £160 per annum.

Figure 115 - Cobbler's Hall Farm, circa 1970s. (Photo courtesy of Ian Robertson via Facebook and originally taken by Ernest Stanley)

Appendix One

Lot 72 – Woodham Grange Farm (Woodham Burn Farm on map). A capital mixed holding of about 192 acres, 3 roods, 24 poles bounded by a brook and with long road frontage to Burn Lane. This stone built and slated farm house has an excellent approach and contains two sitting rooms, kitchen, wash house, five bedrooms, E.C. water from well. The buildings are mainly of stone with tiled roofs and comprise a five stalled stable, good cow house for 11, hay store, Dutch barn, another cow house for 10 with feeding passage, separating room. In Ord. No. 213a is another set of buildings comprising a Cottage of three bedrooms, kitchen, scullery and larder, a stone built cattle shelter, yard, loose box adjoining. The land comprises some excellent grass, some of the fields having frontage to the brook. The plantations and lane Ord. Nos. 221, 204, 198 and part of 202 are in hand. The farm is let on a yearly (13th May) tenancy to Mr. T.W. Lowe at a rental of £120 per annum. The right is reserved to the vendors and their successors in title or assigns to lead timber out of Agnew and South Agnew plantations over the roadway included with this lot.

Lot 73 – A capital little holding known as Well House Farm with excellent frontage to Burn Lane, screened by a belt of timber. The house has a good approach built of stone with pantiled roof and brick chimneys. Sitting room, kitchen, back kitchen, dairy and two bedrooms. Good range of stone and tile buildings including a cow house for 5 or 6, four calf pens, small yard, cow house for young stock, calf pen, loose box, two stall stable. The land is all grass and some of the fields are bounded by the stream. Area about 43 acres, 1 rood, 30 poles. This Lot is let to Mr. J. Johnston on a yearly (13th May) tenancy at £42 per annum.

Figure 116 - Well House Farm (Lot 73) – Photo from Chapman, 1995. (Apparently demolished 1979 – 1980)

Lot 74 – An excellent grass holding of about 65 acres, 0 roods, 38 poles known as Burn House Farm. The homestead is built of stone with a tiled roof and contains sitting room, kitchen, back kitchen, dairy and three bedrooms. Water from well. The buildings include a stone and tiled cow byre for 14, calf house, piggery with loft over, two stall stable, another ditto, rick yard and two bay cart shed with granary over. The land is all grass and has a long frontage to Burn Lane. The spinneys Ord. Nos. 13 and 18 are in hand, the remainder is let to Mr. H.S. Hewitson on a yearly (13th May) tenancy at a rental of £65 per annum. Tithe (commuted value): £3 13s. 5d.

Lot 75 – Burn Hill Farm. Well-situated holding, about 110 acres, 1 rood, 15 poles. Mainly grass, including a stone and pantiled farmhouse containing sitting room, front and back kitchens, pantry, dairy and five bedrooms. Two staircases. Water from spring and a secondary supply from a well. The buildings are mainly of stone with tiled roofs, comprising stabling for 4, chaff house with granary over, good cow house for 11, cattle yard, loose box, two piggeries, small barn, another cow house for 4, calf pen and loose box, Meal House, cart shed and implement shed. This Lot is let to Messrs. Alfred Hawkins and Sons at a rental of £90 per annum on a yearly (13th May) tenancy.

Lot 78 – Pleasantly situated holding of about 157 acres, 0 roods, 28 poles known as Greenfield Farm. Situated in the Parish of Middridge and approached from Middridge Lane. The homestead is built of stone, cement rendered with a slated roof and comprises two sitting rooms, kitchen, dairy, back kitchen, four bedrooms and box room. Drinking water is obtained from a well on the farm. The farm buildings comprise a five bay open cart shed and yard, stone built and pantiled cow byre for 6 with implement shed and six calf pens adjoining, another cow house for 6 with granary over, stable for 5 and two loose boxes. Another stone built cow byre for 10, garage or implement shed, lean-to shed used as piggery and three bay timber Dutch barn. The farm is well watered by a beck. This Lot is let on a yearly (13th May) tenancy to Mr. Henry Valks at a rental of £165 per annum.

Figure 117 - Greenfield Farm (Lot 78) – Photo from Chapman, 1995

Lot 79 – A very attractive small holding including a stone and tiled cottage containing kitchen, back kitchen, bedroom and lumber-room. Water from well. The outbuildings comprise a cow house for 4. The land is all grass and comprises about 10 acres, 1 rood, 32 poles being Ord. Nos. 103, 109, 109a, and part of 110 in the parish of Great Aycliffe. The cottage is occupied by Mrs. Robertson on a life tenancy, rent free. Owner paying rates and being responsible for repairs, and the fields are let to the same tenant on a yearly (13th May) tenancy at £12 per annum. (Authors Note: This Lot is the original cottage at Blue Bells although unnamed in the text it is so named on the Lot map).

Figure 118 - Lot 79 – The original cottage at Blue Bells – used to be at the Middridge exit from Blue Bell Wood (a disused magnesian limestone quarry).

Additional Farms and Cottages
not part of the Eden Estate Sale:

Figure 119 - Low Moor Farm that previously stood across the road from Finchale Cottage Farm. Low Moore Farm survived into the 1950s and can be seen on later photos of the Iron Horse pub that was eventually built across the road in 1953. The farm was still present in late 1955 when Mr. Dent won a prize in the gardens competition. (Photo from Chapman, 1995.)

When Lillian Holmes got married in 1953 she and her husband Ralph moved back into Clarence House (she had lived there earlier as it was her family home) until 1961 when they moved to Church Close. When Clarence House was demolished she removed a few bricks as mementos of her time there (they later lined her fish pond) (Edwards, 1968).

Figure 120 - Clarence Cottages – They stood at the junction of New Lane and the road crossing the Clarence Railway at Simpasture. Apparently they were single story and an upper story was added at a later date. (Photo from Chapman, 1995)

Figure 121 - Simpasture Farm – This farm was where the Oak Leaf Sports Complex stands today (2018) – Photo from 'The Northern Echo, June 10ᵗʰ 2017.

Figure 122 - A very 'grainy' picture taken from an aerial photograph of Bluestone Cottage (Original air photo from Great Aycliffe Town Council dated 14ᵗʰ September 1954) No other photo of Bluestone Cottage is known to exist.

Appendix Two

A List of Businesses with Tenancies on Aycliffe Trading Estate on 30th June 1951. This data was provided by Mr. Sylph (Chairman of the North Eastern Industrial Estates) to Lord Beveridge by his request and transcribed from the original. (spreadsheet continued on following page).

Tenancies on Aycliffe Trading Estate June 1951			
Company	**Factory Area**	**Number of Employees**	**Product Manufactured**
Aycliffe Castings Ltd.	7344	41	Iron Founders
Aycliffe Drum and Kegs Ltd.	8504	21	Metal Containers
Aycliffe Laundry Ltd.	17415	38	Launderers and dry cleaners
Aycliffe Textiles Ltd.	32510	126	Rayon Processing
Bakelite Limited	157544	320	Bakelite and plastic materials
Block and Anderson (Wholesale) Ltd.	49425	180	Office Machinery
Frank Bookless and Co. Ltd.	25138	45	Paints, Enamels, Varnishes, Distempers
Brentwood Metal Industries Ltd.	12658	20	Metal window manufacturer
Celluglos Products	7864	16	Bath panel and glazed wall linings
Chemical Compounds Ltd.	17443	33	Fine chemicals and pharmaceuticals
Combined Plastic Traders (1950) Ltd.	8016	13	Moulders and fabricators of plastic materials
Concordia Electric Wire and Cable Ltd.	12768	34	Insulated wires and cables
Copelaw Engineering Works Ltd.	10777	9	Engineers and machine tool manufacturer
Crowborough Engineering Works	38189	166	Machine tool manufacturers
W.I. Clark	1326	2	Electrical Engineer
Durham County Constabulary	51478	0	County Police Headquarters
East Anglia Chemical Co. Ltd.	26220	172	Pearl and artificial jewellery, blood plasma carried out by subsiduary-Dextran Ltd.
East Anglia Plastics Ltd	26220	68	Plastic moulding powders
East Anglia Lacquer Co.	6000	5	Insulated materials
ENV Engineering Co. Ltd.	35852	52	2 speed axles
W. Gray	5144	12	Joinery Manufacturer
A.J. Hartley & Co. Ltd.	13617	12	Timber poultry houses and packing crates
E. Hammond	1907	1	Caravans
R.V. Hogg & Co.	3025	19	Electrical Engineers
Ideal Doll Ltd.	43259	101	Plastic Dolls
James & Co. (Darlington) Ltd.	5168	4	Butchers outfitters, spice importers
James & Co. (Manufacturers) Ltd.	12261	26	Bedding and Furniture
Kemet Products Ltd.	11667	12	Electric Components for Radar and Transmitters
O. & M. Kleeman Ltd	122454	485	Plastic Fancy Goods
P.B. Kent & Co. Ltd.	14400	17	Agricultural Fertilizer
Leader Paints Ltd.	4627	3	Paints
Lehman, Archer & Lane Ltd.	41043	186	Engineers Tool Makers (Taps and Dies)
Mac Cereals Ltd.	3423	5	Breakfast Cereal and Cereal Confectionary
Mill Coachworks	5424	7	Repairs to bodywork of road vehicles
Mu-Ray Chrome Products	15675	24	Tubular Steel Furniture and Stadium Seating
Paper Converters Ltd.	40705	49	Cardboard Boxes
Pax Paints Ltd.	13101	9	Paints, Enamels, Varnishes and Distempers
Permoid Ltd	15187	36	Metal Bread Bins etc.
Presto Cleaners	1376	2	Cleaners
Remploy Ltd.	9009	37	Disabled Persons Employment Centre
Ridghouse Products Ltd.	7859	16	Metal Greenhouse, Roof Trusses
Rockwell Co. (Darlington) Ltd.	2653	4	Packers and distributors of toilet requisites
C. Rowe	2775	1	Welding

A List of Businesses with Tenancies on Aycliffe Trading Estate on 30th June 1951. (spreadsheet continued from previous page)

Tenancies on Aycliffe Trading Estate June 1951			
Company	**Factory Area**	**Number of Employees**	**Product Manufactured**
C.N. Royle & Co. Ltd.	3033	12	Table lamps and lamp shades
F.L. Saul Ltd.	13871	30	Tinware and metal boxes
Shearex Plastics Ltd.	17372	44	Toolmakers and plastic moulders
Sherwood & Winn Ltd.	27034	47	Coach and Motor body builders
Shrager Bros. Ltd.	21489	98	Furniture Manufacturers
Roy Tallent Ltd.	24121	146	Fine Fancy Goods
Thrislington Engineering Co. Ltd.	8094	9	Engineers
Toledo Woodhead Springs Ltd.	54357	78	Laminated coil springs and accessories for road and rail vehicles
R.W. Toothill Ltd.	12157	36	Furniture Manufacturers
G.A. Willis (Middlesbrough) Ltd.	10792	18	Paints
F.H. Wrigley Ltd.	18174	4	Fillers for plastics
Rediffusion (North East) Ltd.	250	0	Service Station for New Town
Dr. Robson	1080	0	Garage and workshop
F. Rickaby	938	3	Builders
Northern Industrial Finishing Co.	2785	0	Paint finishings
J.W. Gibson	390	2	Post Office
Primula Crispbread Ltd.	3600	0	Crispbread - not yet occupied
Saxton & Co. (London) Ltd.	1217	2	Hirers of plant etc.
Darlington Rural District Council	1134	0	Refuse vehicles - garage
Turner and Ing	1197	5	Quantity Surveyors
Aycliffe Club	729	0	Club Premises
Aycliffe Development Corporation	2890	0	Housing Accommodation
Durham County Civil Defence	4594	7	Civil Defence Office
Martins Bank Ltd.	400	2	
Midland Bank Ltd.	186	2	
National Provincial Bank Ltd.	186	2	
Barclays Bank Ltd.	1008	1	
Lloyds Bank	258	2	
Thos. Bell and Sons	4800	1	Storage
John Binns and Sons	3604	0	Storage
P. Fanghanel & Co. Ltd.	4200	0	Storage
Foundation Oil Co. Ltd.	4680	0	Storage
Machinery Installations Ltd.	11047	0	Storage
J.D. Ord & Co.	11310	0	Storage
H.M. Postmaster General	1340	0	Storage
W. Stanley Robinson & Co.	2349	0	Storage
Tees-Side Farmers Ltd.	11310	0	Storage
North Eastern Electricity Board	12426	0	Storage
F. Sedgwick	182	0	Farming Store
TOTAL		**2980**	

Appendix Three

An Informal 'Census' taken of Newton Aycliffe Residents on 25th May 1951. This was located in the Lord Beveridge Archive at the London School of Economics. Family name; address; number of adults; and age and sex of any children are all shown. Any address that has no family name is presumed unoccupied, likely not complete. The final page of this appendix presents a list of the residents of the pre-existing farms and cottages that were still occupied, but would be demolished over the next few years.

BEV VII 28
(I Vern 10 Pages 1 - B)

LIST OF RESIDENTS – NEWTON AYCLIFFE AS AT 25TH MAY, 1951.

NAMES.	ADDRESS.	ADULTS.	CHILDREN (UNDER 18) SHOWING AGES.	
			MALE	FEMALE
MR. & MRS. F. Hiley.	Breckon House.	2	12,4,1.	14
MRS. L.J. Stevens.	Clarence House.	3	-	-
MR. & MRS. E.W. Bateman.	1, Clarence Green.	2	-	1
" " " J.L. Moore.	2, " "	3	-	12
" " " E. Gray.	3, " "	2	3	-
" " " H. Bilton.	4, " "	2	1	2½
MRS. A.E. Featherstone.	5, " "	2	-	-
MR. & MRS.	6, " "			
" " " J. Lack.	7, " "	2	-	-
" " " K.P. Jackson.	8, " "	2	-	-
" " " J. Perry.	9, " "	2	-	-
" " " W. Charlesworth.	10, " "	2	-	-
" " " J. Hopps.	11, " "	2	3	-
" " " J.R. Hall.	12, " "	2	1	-
MRS. M. M. Nicholson.	13, " "	2	-	-
MR. & MRS. H. Peacock.	14, " "	2	-	-
" " " J.G. Creaney.	15, " "	2	-	-
" " " J.D. Dodsworth.	16, " "	2	-	3
" " " K.C. Corner.	17, " "	2	-	2
" " " A.E. Dixon.	18, " "	2	2	-
" " " D. Oliver.	19, " "	4	-	-
" " " H. Cowie.	20, " "	2	-	6,1.
" " " J.H. Hood.	21, " "	2	-	4,2.
" " " J. Black.	22, " "	2	-	-
" " " F. Connelly.	23, " "	2	-	9
" " " A. Flynn.	24, " "	2	-	3
" " " H. Wilson.	25, " "	2	-	-

NAMES.	ADDRESS.	ADULTS.	CHILDREN (UNDER 18) SHOWING AGES.	
			MALE	FEMALE
MR. & MRS. A. Langlands.	1, TRAVELLERS GREEN.	2	–	4.
" " " A.R. WAILES.	2, " "	2	–	–
" " " J.T. Carey.	3, " "	2	–	3.
" " " D.E.Woodford-Brown	4, " "	2	3.	2.
" " " L. Rand.	5, " "	2	13.	–
" " " L.R. Chaplin.	6, " "	2	8.	–
" " " R. Jones.	7, " "	1) 2)	2.	–
" " " D. Horner.	8, " "	2	–	–
" " " G.A. Dixon.	9, " "	3	–	5.
" " " A.H. Bowes.	10, " "	2	1.	–
" " " G.H. Maffey.	11, " "	2	1.	–
" " " N. Crawford.	12, " "	2	1.	3.
" " " E.W. Tennick.	13, " "	2	–	–
" " " Brierly.	14, " "	2	–	1.
" " " J. Sherlock.	15, " "	2	13,11,4.	–
" " " G. Robson.	16, " "	2	3.	–
" " " A.S. Rowell.	17, " "	2	7.	1.
" " " A.H. Taylor.	18, " "	3	–	–
" " " I. Cotton.	19, " "	3	–	17,10.
" " " A. Stephenson.	20, " "	2	–	3.
" " " T. Nattrass.	21, " "	2	–	3.

Appendix Three

158

NAME.	ADDRESS.	ADULTS.	CHILDREN (UNDER 18) SHOWING AGES.	
			MALE	FEMALE
MR. & MRS. A. Morton.	1, CLARENCE CORNER.	3	-	17.
" " " W.C. Gerrard.	2, " "	2	5.	7.
" " " S. Richardson.	3, " "	2	-	-
" " " E.J. Kerton.	4, " "	2	4.	-
" " " C.R. Atkinson.	5, " "	3	9,15.	-
" " " J.F. Dunn.	6, " "	2	11,12.	4.
" " " E. Hugill.	7, " "	4	16,2.	14,7,6.
" " " R. Marshman.	8, " "	2	7,1.	9,4,2.
" " " R. Slater.	9, " "	2	3.	8.
" " " W. Gray.	10, " "	2	-	17.
" " " B.G. Syrett.	11, " "	2	8.	-
" " " W. Jordison.	12, " "	1	-	-
" " " W. Simpson.	13, " "	2	7.	-
" " " R. Moyle.	14, " "	2	7.	-
" " " J. Simpson.	15, " "	2	3.	-
" " " T.D. Beecroft.	16, " "	2	3.	1.

Appendix Three

159

NAMES.	ADDRESS.	ADULTS.	CHILDREN (UNDER 18) SHOWING AGES.	
			MALE	FEMALE
The Rev. T.E. Drewette.	1, CLARENCE CHARE.	2	-	-
MR. & MRS. R.F. Pettitt.	2, " "	2	14,13.	-
" " " W. Summers.	3, " "	2	1.	-
" " " D. Elkins.	4, " "	2	-	2.
" " " T.W. Wake.	5, " "	2	-	3.
" " " N. Ranson.	6, " "	2	-	2.
" " " F. Priestman.	7, " "	2	-	1.
" " " L. McLeash.	8, " "	2	8.	6.
" " " F. Hood.	9, " "	2	-	-
" " " J.T. Mulholland.	10, " "	2	2.	-
" " " T.V. Teesdale.	11, " "	2	10.	10.
" " " R. Ward.	12, " "	2	-	1.
" " " R. King.	13, " "	2	-	-
" " " J. Hood.	14, " "	2	-	-
" " " H. Bell.	15, " "	3	-	-
" " " R. Morrison.	16, " "	2	-	3.
" " " T. Wilson.	17, " "	2	-	11.
" " " R. Horsley.	18, " "	2	-	-
" " " W. Courtley.	19, " "	2	-	1.
" " " K. Holliday.	20, " "	2	-	2.
" " " B.S.C. Quint.	21, " "	2	-	1.
" " " D. Vickers.	22, " "	2	2.	11.
" " " W. Burns.	23, " "	2	-	4.
" " " E.V. Doughty.	24, " "	2	8.	6.
" " " J.B. Outerside.	25, " "	2	-	-
" " " J.D. Lodge.	26, " "	2	2.	-
" " " D. Houlker.	27, " "	2	8,3,1.	-
" " " G. Wood.	28, " "	2	9.	3.
" " E. Wayman.	29, " "	2	3.	1.
" " C.E. Smith.	30, " "	2	13.	14,10.
R. M. Tooth.	31, " "	1	7,4.	-

Appendix Three

NAME.	ADDRESS.	ADULTS.	CHILDREN (UNDER 18) SHOWING AGES. MALE	FEMALE
MR. & MRS. A.C. Foster.	1, CLARENCE CLOSE.	2	-	-
" " " J.R. Atkinson.	2, " "	2	-	-
" " " A. Morland.	3, " "	4	3,2.	-
" " " W. Falkous.	4, " "	2	-	-
" " " J.D. Brown.	5, " "	2	4.	-
" " " K.R. Johnson.	6, " "	2	2,3.	-
" " " F. Browne.	7, " "	2	-	3.
" " " L. Musgrave.	8, " "	2	-	-
" " " R. Brown.	9, " "	2	-	-
" " " A.E. Holmes.	10, " "	2	-	6,1.

Appendix Three

Appendix Three

NAME.	ADDRESS.	ADULTS.	CHILDREN (UNDER 18) SHOWING AGES.	
			MALE	FEMALE
MR. & MRS. Davison.	1, BALIOL GREEN.	2	6.	1.
" " " J.W. Black.	2, " "	2	4.	–
" " " T.W. Best.	3, " "	3	–	–
" " " W. Gosling.	4, " "	2	–	–
" " " B.V. Northall.	5, " "	2	–	–
" " " B.L. Whitworth.	6, " "	2	–	3.
" " " J.G. Gaul.	7, " "	2	–	–
" " " H.H. Muirhead.	8, " "	2	1 & 1.	–
	9, " "			
	10, " "			
	11, " "			
	12, " "			
	13, " "			
	14, " "			
" " " J.E. Wood.	15, " "	2	–	8.
" " " C.E. Bell.	16, " "	2	–	11.
" " " A. Mafham.	17, " "	2	–	5.
" " " K.W.A. Dorman.	18, " "	2	–	2.
" " " G.E. Barron.	19, " "	2	–	13.
" " " A. Lambert.	20, " "	2	–	2,1.
" " " J.E. Steventon.	21, " "	2	–	–
" " " W.J.W. Hunter.	22, " "	3	–	–
" " " J.E. Middleton.	23, " "	2	8,3.	5.
" " " J.R. Pattison.	24, " "	2	11,9,7.	1.
" " " N. Curry.	25, " "	2	3,2.	–
" " " J.F. Scott.	26, " "	2	–	3.
" " " E. Lee.	27, " "	2	–	3.
" " " R.H. Nicholson.	28, " "	2	15.	–

NAME.	ADDRESS.	ADULTS.	CHILDREN (UNDER 18) SHOWING AGES.	
			MALE	FEMALE
	1, BALIOL ROAD.			
	2, " "			
	3, " "			
	4, " "			
MR. & MRS. S.A.W. Barrass.	5, " "	2	3.	-
" " " R. Bloxsom.	6, " "	2	5.	-
" " " W.E. Johnson.	7, " "	2	-	-
" " " D.J. Mac Donald.	8, " "	2	1.	-
" " " J. Haykin.	9, " "	2	-	1.
" " " W.H. Lovesy.	10, " "	2	1.	-
" " " K.W. Westwood.	11, " "	2	-	4,1.
" " " P. Wade.	12, " "	2	5,2.	7,5.
" " " J.W. Cook.	13, " "	2	-	3.
" " " W.P. Dobson.	14, " "	2	3.	8.

NAME.	ADDRESS.	ADULTS.	CHILDREN (UNDER 18) SHOWING AGES.	
			MALE	FEMALE
MR. & MRS. C.A. Russ.	1, HACKWORTH CLOSE.	2	3.	-
" " " J.W. HUMPHREYS.	2, " "	2	7,8.	-
" " " M.E. Walker.	3, " "	2	-	-
" " " A. Guy.	4, " "	2	-	-
" " " L.F. Robinson.	5, " "	2	-	2.
" " " P. Skerry.	6, " "	2	-	2,1.
" " " M. O'Reilly.	7, " "	2	8,2.	6.
" " " T.W. Whitfield.	8, " "	2	17.	15.
" " " J.R. Taylor.	9, " "	2	5,2.	-
" " " E. Towse.	10, " "	2	-	1.
" " " J.M. Waters.	11, " "	2	6.	1.

Appendix Three

163

NAME.	ADDRESS.	ADULTS.	CHILDREN (UNDER 18) SHOWING AGES.	
			MALE	FEMALE
	1, ANNE SWYFT ROAD.			
MR. & MRS. W. Lewis.	2, " " "	2	-	-
" " "	3, " " "			
" " " W. Bell.	4, " " "	2	-	-
	5, " " "			
" " " T.H. Peacock.	6, " " "	2	1.	-
	7, " " "			
" " " S. Attle.	8, " " "	2	2,1.	-
	9, " " "			
" " " J. Casey.	10, " " "	2	9.	11,2.
	11, " " "			
" " " S. Gildersleeve.	12, " " "	2	-	-
	13, " " "			
" " " J.T. Robinson.	14, " " "	2	3.	-
	15, " " "			
" " " J. Hewitson.	16, " " "	2	-	-
	17, " " "			
" " " F.A. Field.	18, " " "	2	-	-
	19, " " "			
" " " H.L. Robinson.	20, " " "	2	-	8.

NAME.	ADDRESS.	ADULTS.	CHILDREN (UNDER 18) SHOWING AGES	
			MALE	FEMALE
MR. & MRS. J. Nelson.	1, BEDE CRESCENT.	2	1.	-
" " "	2, " "			
	3, " "			
" " " A.B. Westcott.	4, " "	2	-	8.
The Rt. Hon. Lord Beveridge.	5, " "	2	-	-
	6, " "			
	7, " "			
	8, " "			
	9, " "			
	10, " "			
	11, " "			
	12, " "			
	13, " "			
	14, " "			
	15, " "			
	16, " "			
	17, " "			
	18, " "			
	19, " "			
	20, " "			
	21, " "			
	22, " "			
	23, " "			
	24, " "			
	25, " "			
	26, " "			
	27, " "			
	28, " "			
MR. & MRS. E.H.V. Maxted.	29, " "	2	1.	4,3.
MR. & MRS. T.W. Lowe.	30, " "	2	-	-
	31, " "			
	32, " "			

Contd.../

Appendix Three

165

NAME.	ADDRESS.	ADULTS.	CHILDREN (UNDER 18) SHOWING AGES.	
			MALE	FEMALE
	33, BEDE CRESCENT (Contd)			
	34, " "			
	35, " "			
	36, " "			
	37, " "			
	38, " "			
	1, SURTEES WALK.			
	2, " "			
	3, " "			
	4, " "			
MR. & MRS. S. Marshall.	5, " "	2	-	14,17.
" " " N. Waton.	6, " "	2	-	7.
" " " E. Dryden.	7, " "	2	-	1.
" " " S. Tidbury.	8, " "	2	-	10.
MR. & MRS. G.R. Browne.	1, WESTCOTT WALK.	2	-	-
" " " N.R. Holman.	2, " "	2	-	-
" " " E.J. Robinson.	3, " "	2	-	-
" " " H. Thompson.	4, " "	2	8,11.	12.
" " " H. Durell.	5, " "	2	1.	4.
" " " J.R.K. Robson.	6, " "	2	-	-

NAME.	ADDRESS.	ADULTS.	CHILDREN (UNDER 18) SHOWING AGES.	
			MALE	FEMALE
.	1, ELIZABETH BARRETT WALK.			
	2, " " "			
	3, " " "			
	4, " " "			
MR. & MRS. A.E. Barnard.	5, " " "	2	5.	1.
" " " E. Nixon.	6, " " "	2	–	–
" " " T.A. Murray.	7, " " "	3	–	–
" " " C. McDonald.	8, " " "	2	–	5,8.
	9, " " "			
" " " T.J. Gear.	10, " " "	2	–	3.
	11, " " "			
" " " E.R.J. Thomas.	12, " " "	2	–	–
MR. & MRS. W. Clement.	1, HAVELOCK CLOSE.	3	–	14.
" " " F.W. Stone.	2, " "	3	–	–
" " " G. Cooper.	3, " "	2	–	5.
" " " A. Cooling.	4, " "	2	7.	–
" " " W. Watson.	5, " "	3	12,10,5.	15.
" " " E. Grosvenor.	6, " "	2	–	–
" " " S. Wise.	7, " "	2	5,3.	1.
" " " J.L. Martin.	8, " "	2	–	5.

Appendix Three

167

Appendix Three

NAME.	ADDRESS.	ADULTS.	CHILDREN (UNDER 18) SHOWING AGES.	
			MALE	FEMALE
MR. & MRS. J.K. Nattrass.	Finchale Cottage Farm.	2	3.	8.
" " " M. Dent.	Low Moor Farm.	2	-	-
" " " R. Crusher.	Burn House Farm.	2	-	-
" " " D. Jaques.	Sugar Hill Farm.	2	-	-
" " " A. Kidd.	Burn Hill Farm.	2	-	-
Mrs. Johnson.	Well House Farm.			
Walton.	Wellbury House.			
MR. & MRS. LOWE.	Hollins Nook New Lane.			
Lowe.	Woodham Burn.			
Hopps.	Horndale Farm,			
Walton.	William Field Farm.			
Hawkins.				
Mrs. Palmer)				
MR. & MRS. Birch)	1, High Travellers.			
" " " Watson.	2, " "			
" " " Wake.	3, " "			
" " " G. Wake.	4, " "			
" " " Moore.	C/o Hollins Nook, New Lane.			
" " " Bailes.	Railway Cottages.			
" " " Cobb.	Bluestone Cottages.			
" " " E.W. Belfield.	The Lodge.	2	13.	12.
" " " Linton.	4, Clarence Cottages.			
" " " Charlton.	3, Clarence Cottages.			
" " " Lax)				
Mrs. Boddington)	1, Tanyard Cottages.			
Miss Boddington)				
Mr. & Mrs. Everton.	2, Tanyard Cottages.			
" " " P. Timoney.	4, Tanyard Cottages.	2	-	2.

Appendix Four

Individual workers living at Newton Aycliffe, 1950/1951. This is a comprehensive list of early residents that provides detailed information about address; name; spouse's name; children's age and sex; job title; whether working on the trading estate; pay; present rent paid; number of bedrooms; do they want a garage?; is their house electricity or gas?; do they have a washing machine or fridge? The last four pages show 'approved applicants', presumably with no house yet assigned.

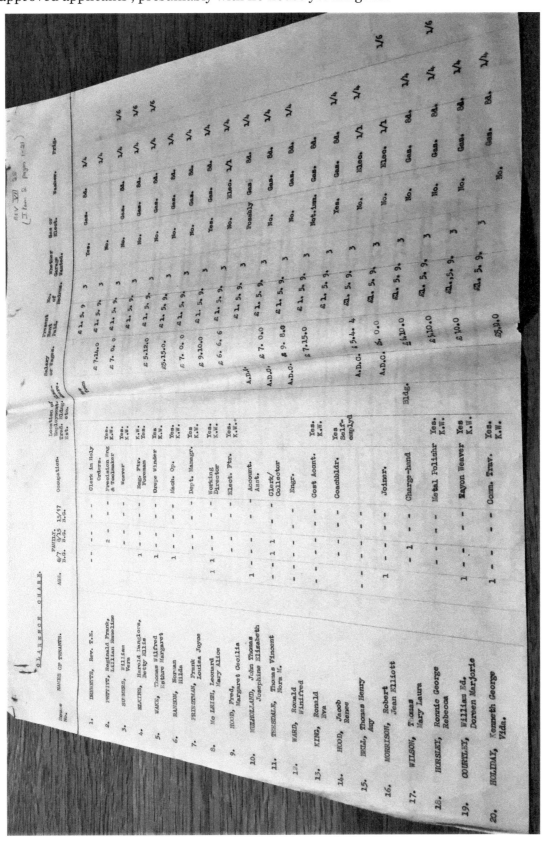

CLARENCE CHARE (CONTD)

House No.	NAMES OF TENANTS.	AGE.	FAMILY. 4/7 B. G.	8/15 B. G.	15/17	Occupation.	Location of Employment Trd. Bldg. Est. etc.	Salary or Wages.	Present Rent Paid.	No. of Bed-rooms.	Whether Garage Wanted.	Gas or Elec.	Washer.	Frig.
21.	QUINT, Basil Stephen Rose Evelyn		- -	1	4	Dept. Supt.	Yes. K.W.		£1.16.1	4	Yes.			
22.	VICKERS, Donald Edna		1 - 1			Bargain Wk. Mining.	Else-where	£11.10.0	£1.16.1.	4	Yes.	Gas	8d.	
23.	BURNS, William		1 - -			Company Sec.	Yes. K.W.	£6. 0.0	£1.16.1.	4	Not im.	Gas	8d.	
24.	DOUGHTY, Eldred Vernon Dora Mary		1 1 -			Supervisor.	Yes. K.W.		£1.16.1.	4	No.			
25.	OUTTERSIDE, John Briggs, Linda		- - -			Bricklayer.	Bldg.	£6.10.0	£1. 9. 7.	3	Yes.	Elec.	1/1	
26.	LODGE, John Duncan Edna Elisabeth		1 - -			Engr. Asst.		A.D.C. £595 p.a.	£1. 9. 7.	3	Yes.	Gas	8d.	1/4
27.	HOULKER, Dennis Sadie		2 - -			Fitter.	Yes. K.W.		£1. 9. 7.	3		Gas	8d.	1/4
28.	WATMAN, Edward Joan		1 1 -			Bricklayer.	Bldg.	£6. 0. 0	£1. 9. 7.	3	No.	Gas	8d.	1/4
29.	WOOD, George Louie		1 1 -			Maintenance Fitter.	Yes. K.W.		£1. 9. 7.	3		Gas	8d.	1/4
30.	SMITH, Charles Eustace.		- 1 2			Joiner.	Bldg. A.D.C.		£1. 9. 7.	3	Yes.	Elec.	1/-	
31.	TOOTH, Runa Minnie		1 - 1			Secretary	A.D.C.	£6.10.0					Elec. 1/-	1/6

CLARENCE CLOSE.

House No.	NAMES OF TENANTS.	AGE. FAMILY. 4/7 8/15 15/17 B.G. B.G. B.G.	Occupation.	Location of Employment. Trd. Ind. etc. Est. etc.	Salary or Wages.	Present Rent Paid.	No. of Bed-Rooms.	Whether Garage Wanted.	Gas. or Elect.	Water.	Frig.
1.	FOSTER, Albert Clifford Ellen Rose	- - -	Tool-shop Foreman	Yes. K.W.	£ 10. 0. 0	£1. 5. 9.	3	Yes.	Gas	8d.	1/4
2.	ATKINSON, James Richard Mary Hattie	- - -	Town & Country Planner. LCC	Elsewhere		£1. 5. 9.	3	Yes.	Gas	8d.	1/4
3.	MORLAND, Alfred Alma	2 - - -	Chief Erector	Yes. K.W.	£600 p.a.	£1. 5. 9.	3	Yes.	Gas	8d.	1/6
4.	FALKOUS, Wilfred Edna May	- - -	Officer-in-C. Civil Defence.	Yes. K.W.		£1. 5. 9.	3	No.	Gas	8d.	1/6
5.	BROWN, John Duston Janet Graham	1 - - -	Instructor Civil Defence.	K.W.	£ 7.15. 0.	£1. 5. 9.	3	Yes.	Gas	8d.	1/6
6.	JOHNSON, Kenneth Robert Cynthia	2 - - -	Technician G.P.O.	Elsewhere K.W.	£ 5.10. 0.	£1. 5. 9.	3	Yes.	Gas	1/-	1/4
7.	BROWN, Francis William	1 - - -	Works Manager.	Trd. Est. K.W.	£ 9.12. 4.	£1.,5. 9.	3		Elec. 1/-	1/-	1/4
8.	MUSGRAVE, Leonard Aubrey	- - -	Tool maker.	Yes. K.W.		£1. 5. 9.	3	Yes.	Gas	8d.	1/4
9.	BROWN, Richard Pamela	- - -	Asst. Arch. & Planner.	G.B. Group.		£1. 5. 9.	3	No.	Gas	8d.	1/6
10.	HOLMES, Arnold Edward Hesta	1 - - -	Joiner.	Yes. K.W.	£ 5.18. 0.	£1. 5. 9.	3	Yes.	Elec. 1/-	Elec. 1/4	1/6

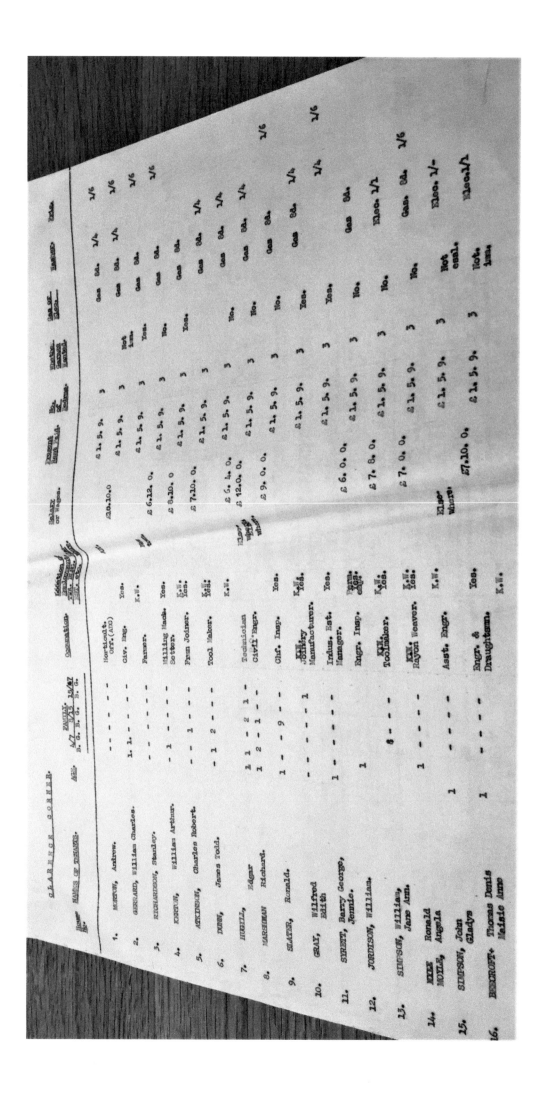

LALIOL GREEN.

House No.	NAMES OF TENANTS.	AGE.	FAMILY. B.G. 6/7 6/15 B.G. 15/17 B.G.	Occupation.	Location of Employment Trade Bldg. Est. etc.	Salary or Wages.	Present Rent Paid.	No. of Bed-Rooms.	Whether Garage Wanted.	Gas. or Elect.	Washer.	Fridge.
1.	DURHAM COUNTY CONSTABULARY.						£4.10.9	3		Gas	8d.	1/1
2.	BLACK, John William / Iris Doreen		– 1 – – –	Experimental Fitter	Yes. K.W.	£6. 0. 0.	£4. 5. 9	3	No.	Elec. 1/1	1/1	1/6
3.	BEST, Thomas Wilfred / Sarah		– – – – –	Warehouse Foreman	Elder where	£5.10. 0	£4. 5. 9	3		Gas	8d.	
4.	GOSLING, Walter / Marjorie		– – – – –	Technical Off. P.O.	Elder where	£5.17. 6.	£4. 5. 9	3	Yes.	Elec. 1/-	1/-	1/6
5.	NORTHALL, Bertram Victor / Winifred May		– – – – –	Technical Off. P.O.	Electric where	£6.10. 0.	£4. 5. 9	3	Yes.	Elec. 1/-		
6.	WHITWORTH, Benjamin Lockit / Mary		1 – – – –	Fitter.	Yes. Perm. empl.	£5. 6. 0.	£4. 5. 9	3	No.	Gas	8d.	
7.	GAUL, John George / Edna		– – – – –	Textiles Weaver	Yes. K.W.	£4.18. 0.	£4. 5. 9	3	Yes.	Gas	8d.	1/1
8.	MUIRHEAD, Hugh Hamilton / Dorothy May		– – – – –	Managing Dir.	Yes. K.W.	£11. 0. 0.	£4. 5. 9	3	Yes.	Elec. 1/-	1/1	1/6
9.												
10.												
11.												
12.												
13.												
14.	WOOD, John Edward / Rose Lillian		– 1 – –	Upholsterer.	Yes. K.W.	Bldg.	£5.19. 9.	£1. 7.11	2	No.	Gas 8d.
5.	BELL, Charles Edward		– 1 – –	Driver-Storekeeper.	Bldg. A.D.C		£1. 7.11	2	No.	Elec. 1/1	
	MAPHAM, Albert / Winifred		1 – – – –	Plasterer	Bldg. A.D.C.		£1. 7.11	2	No.	Gas 8d.
	DORMAN, Kenneth Wm. Alfred / Ivy		1 – – – –	Joiner	Bldg.		£1. 7.11	2	No.	Gas 8d.
	BARRON, George Edward / Doris		– – – 1 – –	Clerk of Wks.	Bldg. A.D.C.		£1. 7.11	2	No.	Gas 8d.
	ALBERT, Albert / Florence		1 – – – – –	Foreman Joiner. Yes. K.W.		£6.14. 0.		2	No.	Gas 8d.

B A L I O L   G R E E N (C.NTD).

House No.	NAMES OF TENANTS.	AGE. 4/7 B.G.	FAMILY. 8/15 B.G.	15/17 B.G.	Occupation,	Location of Employment, Trad. Bld.&Elso Est. etc. where.	Salary or Wages.	Present Rent Paid.	No. of Bed-Rooms.	Whether Garage Wanted.	Gas. or Elect.	Washer.	Frig.
21.	STEVENSON, James Edward / Selina				Millwright	Yes. K.W.	£ 6.14.6.	£1.7.11	2	No.	Gas	8d.	
22.	HUNTER, William John Watson / Louise	1	1	1	Plasterer	Bldg.	£ 6.6.6.	£1.7.11	2		Gas	8d.	
23.	MIDDLETON, James Edward / Gladys	1	3		Plasterer	Bldg.		£1.9.7.	3	No.	Gas	8d.	
24.	PATTISON, John Robert / Renee	2			Bricklayer	Bldg		£1.9.7.	3	No.	Gas	8d.	
25.	CURRY, Norman / Annie	1			Carpenter	Bldg		£1.9.7.	3	No.	Elec. 1/1		
26.	SCOTT, John Frederick / Freda				Storekeeper	Else-where		£1.9.7.	3		Gas 8d.		1/1
	LEE, Edwin / Violet					Yes. K.W.		£1.9.7.	3				
	NICHOLSON, Reginald Henry / Eleanor Ada	1			Foreman			£1.9.7.	3	No.			

BALIOL ROAD.

House No.	NAMES OF TENANTS.	AGE. Family. W/7 0/15 15/17 B.G. B.G. B.G.	Occupation.	Location of Employment. Truck Miles. Etc.	Salary or Wages.	Present Rent Paid.	No. of Bedrooms.	Washer Group Wanted.	Gas or Elec.	Washer.	Frig.
1.											
2.											
3.											
4.											
5.	BARRABB, Stanley A.W. Marya P.F.	- - - - 1 -	Despatch Foreman.	Yes. K.W.	£ 6.10. 0.	£1. 5. 9.	3	No.	Gas 8d.		
6.	BLOXSON, John Christopher, Mary Elisabeth	- - - 1 - -	Joiner.	Yes. K.W.	£ 6. 5. 0.	£1. 5. 9.	3	No.	Gas 8d.		
7.	JOHNSON, William Edward, Rina Eveline	- - - - - -	Van Driver.	Yes. K.W.	£ 6. 0. 0.	£1. 5. 9.	3	No.	Gas 8d.	1/6	
8.	McDONALD, Dixon Joseph, Iris	- - - - - -	Rayon Creper.	Yes. K.W.	£ 5.12. 0.	£1. 5. 9.	3	No.	Gas 8d.	1/6	
9.	HAMLIN, John, Maisie	- - - - - -	Sheet Metal Worker.	Yes. K.W.	£ 6. 0. 0.	£1. 5. 9.	3	No.	Gas 8d.	1/4	1/6
10.	LOVESEY, William Henry, Joan	- - - - - -	Standards Eng.	Yes. K.W.	£ 7. 0. 0.	£1. 5. 9.	3	Yes.	Gas 8d.	1/4	1/6
11.	WESTWOOD, Kenneth Walter, Joan Elisabeth	2 - - - - -	Quantity Surveyor.	Yes. K.W.	£ 8.10. 0.	£1. 5. 9.	3	Yes.	Gas 8d.	1/4	
12.	WADE, Frederick, Ella	1 2 - - - -	Resident Maintenance Engr.	Yes. K.W.	£ 6.12. 0.	£1. 5. 9.	3	No.	Elec. 1/1	1/4	1/6
13.	COOK, John Wilson, Ada	1 - - - - -	Toolroom Turner.	Yes. K.W.	£ 6. 4. 8.	£1. 5. 9.	3	No.	Gas 8d.	1/4	1/6
14.	DOBSON, William Paul, Anne	1 2 - - - -	Wood Machinist.	Yes. K.W.							1/6

HACKWORTH CLOSE.

House No.	Names of Tenants	Age 4/7 B.G.B.	Family 8/15 B.G.	15/17 B.G.	Occupation	Location of Employment. Trad. Eld. Est. etc.	Elsewhere	Salary or Wages	Present Rent Paid	No. of Bedrooms	Whether Garage Wanted	Gas or Elect.	Washer	Frig.
1.	RUSS, Charles Arthur / Kathleen Rosina	1	-	-	Metal Polish-er	Yes. K.W.		£ 5.17.4.	£ 1. 5. 9.	3	No.	Gas 8d.	1/4	1/6
2.	HUMPHREYS, John William / Audrey	-	2	-	Steel Partit-ion Worker	Yes. K.W.		£ 6. 0. 0.	£ 1. 5. 9.	3	No.	Gas 8d.	8d.	
3.	WALKER, Malcolm E. / Mary	-	-	-	Asst. to Wks. Manager.	Yes. K.W.		£ 6. 0. 0.	£ 1. 5. 9.	3	No.	Elec. 1/1	8d.	1/4
4.	GUY, Albert / Norah	1	-	-	Toolmaker. Foreman.	Yes. K.W.		£ 8. 8. 6.	£ 1. 5. 9.	3	No.	Gas 8d.	8d.	
5.	ROBINSON, Leslie Fraser / Elsie	1	-	-	Upholsterer Chargehand	Yes. K.W.		£ 7. 8. 0.	£ 1. 5. 9.	3	No.	Gas 8d.	8d.	1/4
6.	SKERRY, Peter / Gladys	1	-	-	Toolroom Foreman.	Yes. K.W.		£ 8. 5. 0.	£ 1. 5. 9.	3	No.	Gas 8d.	8d.	1/4
7.	O'Reilly Michael / Lily	1	1	1	Sewage Labr. Darlington RDC		Else-where.	£ 5. 5. 0.	£ 1. 9. 7.	3		No.	8d.	
8.	WHITFIELD, Thomas William / Mary Ann	-	1	-	Spray Shop Foreman	Yes. K.W.		£ 6. 3. 9.	£ 1. 9. 7.	3		No.	8d.	
9.	TAYLOR, John Robert / Gladys	2	-	-	Process Wkr.	Yes. K.W.		£ 5. 0. 0.	£ 1. 9. 7.	3		No.	Elec. 1/1	
10.	TOWSE, Ernest / Doreen	1	-	-	Foundry Wkr	Yes. K.W.		£ 6. 6. 0.	£ 1. 9. 7.	3		No.	Gas 8d.	
11.	WATERS, Marjorie Jack Money / Marjorie	1	1	-	Machine Shop Foreman.	Yes. K.W.		£ 8.10. 0.	£ 1. 9. 7.	3		No.	Elec. 1/1	

ANNE SWIFT ROAD.

House No.	NAMES OF TENANTS.	AGE. 4/7 B.G.	FAMILY. 15/17 B.G.B.G.	Occupation.	Location of Employment. Trad.,Dist., Est. etc. Else-where.	Salary or Wages.	Present Rent Paid.	No. of Bed-rooms.	Whether Garage Wanted.	Gas or Elect.	Washer.	Fridge.
2.	LEWIS, William Clara	-	-	Bricklayer	Bldg.	£5.2.0.	£1.5.9.	3	Yes.	Gas 8d.	1/4	1/4
4.	BULL, William Mary Agnes	-	-	Foreman Gardener.	Trad. Est. K.W.	£5.0.6.	£1.5.9.	3	No.	Gas 8d.	1/4	1/4
6.	PEACOCK, Thomas Alfred	-	-	Operator.	Trad. Est. K.W. Yes K.W.	£7.0.0.	£1.5.9.	3	No.	Gas 8d.	1/4	1/6
8.	ATTLE, Stanley Mary Edna	1	-	Polisher.		£6.2.0.	£1.5.9.	3	Yes.	Gas 8d.	1/4	
10.	CASSY, Hilda John	1 1 1	-	Plasterer.	Bldg.	£8.10.0.	£1.5.9.	3	No.	Gas 8d.	1/4	
12.	GILBERSLEWS, Stanton Joan	-	-	Bricklayer	Bldg.	£6.0.0.	£1.5.9.	3	Yes.	Gas 8d.	1/4	1/6
14.	ROBINSON, Gerard Thomas Elizabeth	1	-	Joiner.	Bldg.	£6.2.10.	£1.5.9.	3	No.	Gas 8d.		
16.	HEWTNSON, Joseph Margaret Jane	1	-	Process Wkr.	Yes K.W.	£6.10.0.	£1.5.9.	3	No.	Else. 1/-	5th 1/4	1/4
18.	FIELD, Frederick Arthur Dorothy	-	-	Bricklayer	Bldg.	£7.10.0.	£1.5.9.	3	No.	Else. 1/-	1/4	1/4
20.	ROBINSON, Leslie Herbert	1	-	Internal Auditor.	Else-where	£10.0.0.	£1.7.1.	3	No.	Gas 8d.	1/4	

1.

BIRCHGREEN.

House No.	NAMES OF TENANTS	AGE	FAMILY A/T 6/15 15/17 B.G. B.G. B.G.	Occupation	Location of Employment Trad. Est.	Salary or Wages	Present Rent Paid	No. of Bed-rooms	Shelter Garage Wanted.	Gas. or Elec.	Water.	Pets.
1.	Nelson, Joseph Mark		1 - - - - -	Internal Auditor		A.D.G.	£30. 0. 0.	£1 11. 1	2.	No.	Gas.	Gas 8d.	2/6
2.													
3.	WESTCOTT, Alan Hilgh		- - - - 2 -	District Manager	Trad. Est.		£2. 9. 9.	4		Yes.	Gas 8d.	Gas 8d.	
4.	Ellen		- - - - - -	Author & Economist		A.D.G.	£2. 13. 4.	4		Yes.	Gas 8d.	Gas 8d.	
5.	BEVERIDGE, Lord (William) Lady (Janet)												
6.													
7.													
8.													
9.													
10.													

11/28 SCHINDLER GARDEN FLATS (SEPARATE SHEET).

House No.	NAMES OF TENANTS	AGE	FAMILY	Occupation	Location of Employment Trad. Est.	Salary or Wages	Present Rent Paid	No. of Bed-rooms	Shelter Garage Wanted.	Gas. or Elec.	Water.	Pets.
29.	MAXTED, Ethelbert Henry Vinat, Lillian		- 3 - - - -	Painter & Decorator.	Bldg.	A.D.G.		£ 1. 5. 9.	3	No.	Gas 8d.		
30.	LOWE, Thomas William		- - - - - -	Retired Farmer.				£ 1. 5. 9.	3	Yes.	Elec. 1/-		2/6
31.													
32.													
33.													

HAVELOCK CLOSE.

House No.	NAMES OF TENANTS.	AGE.	FAMILY. U/7 B.G.	8/15 B.G.	15/17 B.G.	Occupation.	Location of Employment; Trad., Place, Inst., etc.	Salary or Wages.	Present Rent Paid.	No. of Bed-rooms.	Whether Garage Wanted.	Gas. or Elect.	Washer.	Fri.Ad.
1.	CLEMSON, Wilfred Catherine.		- -	x 1	- -	Clerk of Wks.	A.D.C.	£9.0.0	£1. 5. 9.	3	No.	Gas 8d.		1/6
2.	SHORE, Frederick William Mary		- -	- -	- -	Wks. Foreman	Yes. K.W.	£7.0.0.	£1. 5. 9.	3	No.			
3.	COOPER, Gilbert Eastwood		1 -	- -	- -	Planning Asst.	B.R. Group.		£1. 5. 9.	3	Yes.	Elec. 1/-	1/4	
4.	COLING, Albert		1 -	- -	- -	Machine Fore-man	Yes. K.W.	£5. 6. 0.	£1. 5. 9.	3	No.	Elec. 1/-		
5.	WATSON, William		1 -	2 -	- 1	Bricklayer	Bldg	£6. 2. 6.	£1. 5. 9.	3	No.	Elec. 1/-		
6.	GROSVENOR, Edward Mary		- -	- -	- -	Bricklayer	Bldg	£6.10. 0.	£1. 5. 9.	3	No.	Gas 8d.		
7.	WISE, Stanley Margaret	3 1	- -	- -	- -	Clerk.(Bldg)	A.D.C.		£1. 5. 9.	3	No.	Elec. 1/-	1/4	1/6
8.	MARTIN, John Laurie		- 1	1 -	- -	Clerk of Wks.	A.D.C.	£9. 4. 0.	£1. 5. 9.	3	No.	Gas 8d.		

SURTEES WALK

House No.	NAMES OF TENANTS.	AGE.	FAMILY. U/7 B.G.	8/15 B.G.	15/17 B.G.	Occupation.	Location of Employment; Trad., Place, Inst., etc.	Salary or Wages.	Present Rent Paid.	No. of Bed-rooms.	Whether Garage Wanted.	Gas. or Elect.	Washer.	Fri.Ad.
1.														
2.														
3.														
4.														
5.	MARSHALL, Sydney Edith		- -	- -	- 1	Site Foreman	Bldg. A.D.C.	£7.15. 0.	£1. 5. 9.	3	No.	Elec. 1/-	No.	EM
6.	EATON, Norman Ellen		- -	- 1	- -	Flour Van Salesman.	Yes. K.W.	£10. 0. 0.	£1. 5. 9.	3	No.	Gas 8d.	No.	1/6
7.	DRYDEN, Eric Catherine		- 1	- -	- -	Plumber	Bldg.	£6. 8. 6.	£1. 5. 9.	3	No.	Gas 8d.	No.	1/6
8.	TILBURY, Charles Gardner Hannah		- -	- 1	- -	Shop Manager	New Town	£6. 0. 0.	+£6.1. 5. 9.	3	No.	Gas 8d.	No.	1/6

ELIZABETH BARRETT WALK.

House No.	NAMES OF TENANTS.	AGE. PAILY. 4/7 6/25 13/17 Nr. G. B. G. G. B. G.	Occupation.	Location of Employment. Trade etc. Est. etc.		Salary or wages.	Present Rent paid.	No. of Bedrooms.	Whether Grouped controls.	Gas or Water. Elec.	Rate.
1.											
2.											
3.											
4.	BARNARD, Anthony Stimpll / Kathleen Laura	1 1 - - - -	Works Mangr	Yes. N.W.			£1.12.5.	3	Yes.	Gas 8d.	
5.	NIXON, Eli / Vera	- - -	Bricklayer	Bdg.		£6.11.9	£1.5.9.	3	No.	Gas 8d.	
6.	MURRAY, Thomas Alan / Ethel Maud	- - -	Mang. Dir.	Yes. N.W.		£12.0.0	£1.18.5.	3	Yes.	Gas 8d.	
7.	McDONALD, Claude	1 - 1 -	Carpenter & Joiner.	Bdg.		£6.5.0	£1.5.9.	3	No.		
8.											
10.	GEAR, Thomas James / Edith Mary	2 -	Engr. Wks. Foreman	Yes. N.W.		£6.10.0	£1.5.9.	3	No.	Elec 1/-	
12.	THOMAS, Ernest Reginald John / Joan	- - -	Architect.			G.B. Group £9.10.0	£1.5.9.	3	No.	Gas 8d.	1/6

WESTCOTT WALK.

House No.	NAMES OF TENANTS.	AGE.	Occupation.			Salary or wages.	Present Rent paid.	No. of Bedrooms.	Whether Grouped controls.	Gas or Water. Elec.	Rate.
1.	BROWN, George Robert	- - - -	Architect.			A.D.C. Grad.V.	£1.5.9.	3	No.	Gas 8d.	1/6
2.	HOLMAN, Norman Robert / Joan Margaret	- - - -	Architect.			A.D.C.	£1.5.9.	3	No.	Elec 1/1	1/4
3.	ROBINSON, Edmund J. / Helen	- - -	Architect			G.B. Group	£1.19.2.	3	Yes.		1/4
4.	THOMSON, Hilton / Isabella	- 2 1	Bldg. Manager			A.D.C. Grade VIXIL.19.2.	£1.5.9	3	Yes.	Elec 1/-	1/4
5.	DURELL, Harry	1 1 - - -	Architect			A. D. C. £13.13.0		3	No.	Gas 8d.	1/4
6.	ROBSON, John Robert Keith / Sybil.	- - - -	Medical Practioner			New Town	£1.5.9.	3	Yes.		1/4

CLARANCE GREEN. (ALUMINIUM BUNGALOWS.)

House No.	NAMES OF TENANTS.	AGE.	FAMILY. 4/7 B.G.	8/15 B.G.	15/17 B.G.	Occupation.	Location of Employment. Twn. Bldg. Est. etc.	Else-where.	Salary or Wages.	Present Rent Paid.	No. of Bed-Rooms.	Whether Garage Wanted.	Gas or Elec.	Yes.	Built in
1.	BARNHAM, Karl Walshaw / Evelyn Mary.					Engineer.		A.B.C.	£6.15.0.	£1. 0. 0.	2		Gas.	1/4	"
3.	GREY, Albert Edward / Florence May.		1			Wood Machinist	Yes. K.W.			£1. 0. 0.	2	No	Elec.	1/4	"
5.	FEATHERSTONE, Amy E.						Yes. K.W.			£1. l. l.	2		Elec.	1/4	"
7.	LACK, James Arthur / Alice Ann					Foreman Palmer	Yes. K.W.			£1. l. l.	2			1/4	"
9.	FERRY, Donald George / Evelyn Turner		1			Production Controller	Yes. K.W.			£1. l. l.	2			1/4	"
11.	HOPPS, Harry					Miner		Else-where.	£7. 0. 0.	£1. l. l.	2	No.		1/4	"
13.	NICHOLSON, Margaret M.					Private Sec.	Yes. K.W.		£10.12.0	£1. l. l.	2	Yes.		1/4	"
15.	GREANEY, James Grant / Eva					Caster	Yes. K.W.			£1. l. l.	2			1/4	"
17.	EKNER, Kenneth Charles / Lorna Isabel					Welder	Yes. K.W.			£1. l. l.	2			1/4	"
19.	OLIVER, Joseph William / Jennie Marion					Turner	Yes. K.W.			£1. l. l.	2			1/4	"
21.	HOOD, Joseph Henry														
23.	CONNELLY, Frank / Mabel		1			Bldg. Surveyor	Yes. K.W.		G.R. Grp.	£1. 0. 0. £1. l. l.	2	No	Elec.	1/4	"
25.	WILSON, Henry / Margaret					Aluminium Technician	Yes. K.W.			£1. l. l.	2			1/4	"
2.	MOORE, Joseph Leslie / Kathleen Irene		-)	1		Secretary.	Yes. K.W.		A.D.O.	£1. l. l.	2			1/4	"
4.	BILTON, Harry / Grace		1			Committee Clerk.			A.B.C.	£1. l. l.	2			1/4	"
6.	ROWELL, Arthur Surtees / Dorothy Jean					Draughtsman.				£1. l. l.	2			1/4	"
8.	JACKSON, Kenneth Peter / Veronica					Despatch Clerk	Yes. K.W.			£1. l. l.	2			1/4	"
10.	CHARLESWORTH, William / Joyce					Maintenance Fitter.	Yes. K.W.		A.B.C.	£7.15.0. £1. l. l.	2	Yes		1/4	"
12.	HALL, John Rupert					Eng'r. Asst.									

Appendix Four

CLARENCE GREEN (CONTD.)

House No.	NAMES OF TENANTS.	AGE. 4/7 B.G.	FAMILY. 8/15 B.G.	15/17 B.G.	Occupation.	Location of Employment. Trad. Bldg. Est. etc. Elsewhere.	Salary or Wages.	Present Rent Paid.	No. of Bed-Rooms.	Whether Garage Wanted.	Gas or Elec.	Washer.	Frig.
14.	PEACOCK, Hubert Emie	-	-	-	Maintenance Foreman	Yes. K.W.		£1. 1. 1.					1/4
16.	DODSWORTH, John George Doreen	1	-	-	Electric Welder.	Yes. K.W.		£1. 1. 1.				1/4	
18.	DIXON, Francis William Elsie	-	-	-	Plastic Moulder.	Yes. K.W.		£1. 1. 1.					1/4
20.	COWIE, Henry Irene	1	-	-	Painter	Yes. K.W.		£1. 1. 1.					1/6
22.	BLACK, Doris							£1. 1. 1.					1/4
24.	FLINN, Joseph Vera.	1	-	-	Process Worker.	Yes. K.W.		£1. 1. 1.					

TRAVELERS' GLEN.

House No.	NAMES OF TENANTS.	AGES. FAMILY. 4/7 B.G.	8/15 B.G.	15/17 B.G.	Occupation.	Location of Employment. Trad. Bldg. Est. etc.	Else-where.	Salary or Wages.	Present Rent Paid.	No. of Bed-rooms.	Whether Garage Wanted.	Gas ro Elec.	Washer.	Frig.
18	TAYLOR, Alexander Herbert	- -	- -	-	Bricklayer.	Bldg.	A.D.C.		£1. 9. 8.	3	No.		Gas.	
17.		- -	1 -	1	Painter.	Bldg.	A.D.C.	£6. 5. 0.	£1.12. 0	3	No.		Gas.	
19.	COTTON, Irving Ivy	- 1	- -	- -	Toolmaker.	Trad.	K.W.	£7.15. 0.	£1. 9. 0.	3	No.		Elec.	
20.	STEPHENSON, Alan Elisabeth	- -	- -	- -	Production Manager.	Yes.	K.W.	£9. 0. 0.	£1. 9. 8.	3	No.		Gas.	
21.	NATTRASS, Thomas Mary.	- 1	- -	- -					£1.12. 0.					

TENANTS' GUIDE (ALUMINIUM BUNGALOWS)

House No.	NAMES OF TENANTS.	AGE. A/7 B.G.	8/15 B.G.	15/17 B.G.	FAMILY	Occupation.	Location of Employment. Trd., Fldg. Est. etc.	Salary or Wages.	Present Rent Paid.	No. of Bed-rooms.	Winter Group Rental.	Gas or Elec.	Washer.	Frig.
1.	LANGAINE, Albert / Margaret Una.	1	- -	- -		Designer.	Yes. K.W.		£1.1.1.				1/4	
2.	WALKER, Arthur Ridley / Jean.		- -	- -		Clerk.	Yes. K.W.		£1.1.1.				1/4	
3.	CAREY, John Thomas / Grace Marjorie	1	- -	- -		Rayon weaver.	Yes. K.W.		£1.1.1.					1/4
4.	WOODWARD-BROWN, David Edwin / Jessie	1	- -	- -		Engineering Fitter.	Yes. K.W.		£1.1.1.					1/4
5.	RAND, Laurence / Gladys Hazel		- -	1			Yes. K.W.	£6.19.0	£1.1.1.					
6.	CHAPLIN, Leonard Robert / Jean	1	- -	- -		Fitter and Mounter.	Yes. K.W.		£1.1.1.					
7.	JONES, Ronald / Dorothy	1	- -	- -		Coach & Body Bldr.	Yes. K.W.		£1.1.1.					
8.	HORNER, Dennis / Margaret		- -	- -		Electrician.	Yes. K.W.		£1.1.1.					
9.	DIXON, George Archibald / Kathleen Barbara	1	- -	- -		Good Yard Foreman.	Else-where.		£1.1.1.					
10.	BOWES, Allan Hodgson / Petronella Hendrica		- -	- -		Sheet Metal Worker.	Yes. K.W.	Bldg.	A.D.C.	£1.1.1.		No.		1/4
11.	HAPPEY, George H. / Joan Mary	1	- -	- -		Joiner.	Yes. K.W.	A.D.C.	£1.1.1.		No.		1/6	
12.	CRAWFORD, Norman	1	- -	- -		Production Man	Yes. K.W.		£1.1.1.					
13.	TENNICK, Ernest W. / Doreen		- -	- -		Gardener.	A.D.C.	£7.0.0	£1.1.1.		No.		1/4	
14.	DURHAM COUNTY CONSTABULARY.													
15.	SHERLOCK, John / Doris	1	2 -	- -		Driver, Chargehand Plumber.	A.D.C.	£5.0.0	£1.1.1.		A.D.C.		1/4	
16.	ROBSON, George / Lily	1	- -	- -		Office Manager.	Yes. K.W.		£1.1.1.				1/4	

APPROVED APPLICANTS.

NAMES OF APPLICANTS.	AGES. FAMILY. 4/7 B.G.	6/15 B.G.	15/17 B.G.	Occupation.	Location of Employment. Trad. Bldg. Est. etc.	Elsewhere.	Salary or Wages.	Present Rent Paid.	No. of Bedrms reqd.	Whether Garage wanted.	Gas or Elec.
TAYLOR, Henry.				Arch. Asst.		A.D.O.	£20. 0. 0.		2		Either
GREENALL, John.				Machinist.	Yes. K.W.		£17.17. 5.	8/6	2	No.	Gas.
AINSWORTHY, Harry.	1			Toolmaker.	Yes. K.W.		£7.13. 0	10/-	2.	Yes.	Either.
GILL, Reginald.				Cellulose Sprayer.	Yes. K.W.		£6. 0. 0.	15/-	2.	No.	Either.
BROWN, Harry.	1			Maintenance Electrician	Yes. K.W.		£7. 3. 0.		2.	No.	Elec.
BOLTON, Joseph Edward.	1			Creper.	Yes. K.W.		£6. 5. 0.	6/5	2	No.	Gas.
HUTTON, Ernest Wheatley.				Instructor. Machine Setter.	Yes. K.W.		£5.10. 0.		2.	No.	Either.
WILSON, Ernest.				Press Operator	Yes. K.W.		£5.15. 0.		2.	No.	Elec.
BROWN, Michael Robert.				Sheet Metal Wkr.	Yes. K.W.		£ 7.10.0	8/-	2.	No.	Elec.
LYNCH, William.				Maintenance Fitter.	Yes. K.W.		£6. 7. 0.		2.	No.	Gas.
DENTON, Frederick.	1			- do -	Yes. K.W.		£6.10. 0	7/6	2.	No.	Gas.
DAVIS, Joseph William				Inspection Depot.	Yes. K.W.		£5.10. 0.	8/-	2.	No.	Gas.
KAVANAGH, Paul James.				Maintenance Fitter.	Yes. K.W.		£ 6. 6.0.		2.	No.	Elec.
YAXLEY, William Henry.				Charge of Progess.	Yes. K.W.		£11. 0.0	10/-	2.	No.	Gas.
YOUNG, Joseph MacGregor.				Manager.	Yes.	Big.		30/-	2.	Yes.	Elec.
RIDLEY, Robert.				Bricklayer.			£7. 2.0		2.	No.	Elec.
STEELE, John.	1			Administr.	Yes. K.W.		£8. 0.0.		2.	Not imm.	Elec.
TOWNSEND, Geoffrey Malcolm.				Quantity Surveyor.	Yes. K.W.		£10.10.0	52/6	2.	Yes.	Elec.
SHERBOURNE, Edward Frank Henry				Chemist.	Yes. K.W.		£10. 0.0		2.	No.	Gas.
JOHNSON, Stanley.		1		Colliery Official		Elsewhere.	£12.1. 0.	Free.	2.	Yes.	Either.

185

NAMES OF APPLICANTS.	AGES. FA/TAX 4/7 /13 10/27 B.C. S.C. F.C.	Occupation.	Location of Employment. Trad. Else. etc. where.	Salary or Wages.	Present Rent Paid.	No. of Bed-rooms reqd.	Whether Garage wanted.	Gas. or Elec.
LAMB, Robert Ramley.	1 1 - 1 -	Fitter.	Yes. Farm.	£6. 0. 0.	15/11	3.	No.	Gas.
PICKARD, Harry.	- 2 - - -	Labour Off.	Yes. K.W.		15/-	3	Yes.	Gas.
HALL, Frederick Ronald.	1 - - - -	Textile Foreman.	Yes. K.W.		8/10	3	No.	Either.
DAVIS, Arthur.	1 - - - -	Inspector.	Yes. K.W.	£7. 4. 0	30/-	3.	Yes.	Gas.
AUSTIN, Sidney.	1 - - 1 -	Lab. Supr.	Yes. K.W.	£8. 0.0	7/-	3.	No.	Elec.
SUTTON, Frederick James.	1 - - - -	Attendant. Animl.	Yes. K.W.	£7. 0.0		3.	No.	Elec.
McTEAGUE, George Walter.	1 - 1 - -	Chemists Asst.	Yes. K.W.	£6.10.0	5/-	3.	No.	Gas.
STAVELEY, Wilfred.	- 1 1 - -	Mill Opr.	Yes. K.W.	£6. 0.0	5/-	3.	No.	Elec.
HALLIWELL, Charles Douglas.	1 - - - -	Toolmaker.	Yes. K.W.	£7.10.0		3.	Yes.	Elec.
WILLIAMS, William Benn.	- - - - -	Chemist.	Yes. K.W.	£10.10.0	45/-	3.	No.	Gas.
KNIGHT, Edward Percy.	1 1 - - -	Toolmaker.	Yes. K.W.	£8.15.0	8/10	3.	No.	Either.
GREENWOOD, Ronald Estbury.	- 2 - - -	Wks. Mangr.	Yes. K.W.	£12.0.0	52/-	3.	No.	Gas.
FRANKLEY, William Leacont.	- 1 - - -	Foreman.	Yes. K.W.	£3. 0.0	9/10	3.	No.	Elec.
ROGERS, William Charles.	1 - 2 - -	Wks. Mangr.	Yes. K.W.	£12.10.0	30/-	3.	Yes.	Either.
CLARK, Leonard.	- - - - -	Maintenance Fn.	Yes. K.W.	£7. 5.0	9/-	3.		Elec.
GILDERAN, George Albert.	- - 1 - -	Architect.	A.D.O.			3.		
McNALES, Kenneth Leonard.	- 1 - - -	Lab. Asst.	Yes. K.W.	£5.15.0		3.	No.	Gas.
MITCHELL, Trevor.	1 - - - -	Electrician.	Yes. K.W.	£7.12.0	20/-	3.	No.	Gas.
WELLS, John.	1 - - - -	Charge Nurse.	Else-where.	£10.0.0	Free.	3.	No.	Elec.
NICHOLSON, John Riddlecombe	- - - - -	Miner.	Else-where.	£10.0.0		3.	No.	Elec.

NAMES OF APPLICANTS.	APPROVED APPLICANTS. AGES. 4/7 B.G.	8/15 B.G.	16/17 B.G.	FAMILY	Location of Employment. Trdg. Bldg. Est.	Elsewhere.	Occupation.	Salary or Wages.	Present Rent Paid.	No. of Bedrooms reqd.	Whether Garage wanted.	Gas or Elec.
DIXON, Alfred Henry.	-	-	-	-		Elsewhere.	Rep. Insurance.	£10.0.0 +	50/-	3.	Yes.	Elec.
COYNE, Wilfred Herman.	- 1 1	-	-	-	Yes. K.W.		Coach Pntr.	£3.15.0	20/-	3	No.	Elec.
HATHETON, Ernest.	1 1	-	-	-	Yes. K.W.		Boilerman.	£6.0.0	18/6	3	No.	Either.
HOBBS, Leslie John.	- 1	-	1	-	Yes.		Inspector.	£6.3.0	11/11	2	No.	Gas.
MARLOW, John.	-	-	-	-		Elsewhere.	Clerk.	£9.0.0	x1	3.	Yes.	Elec.
BIRCH, Reginald.	1	-	-	-	Yes. K.W.		Lithographer.	£10.0.0.		3.	Yes.	Gas.
LING, Cecil Howard.	-	-	-	-		Elsewhere.	Distribution Engr.(Yes)	£5.0.0.		2.	2/3	Gas.
HORNER, William.	E-					E.R.G.	Gen. Foreman.	£8.0.0.	30/-	2	2	Either.
WILLIAMSON, William David.	-	-	-	-	Yes. K.W.		Lithographer.	£12.0.0.	50/-	2.	No.	Elec.
STOKES, William.	-	-	-	-	Yes. K.W.		Steel Partition Maker.	£5.11.4	8/-	2.	No.	Elec.
HARMER, Bertram John.	1 1 1	-	-	-	Yes. K.W.		Machine Op.	£4.15.0	8/-	2.	No.	Elec.
KELL, Robert.	-	-	-	-	Yes. K.W.		Maintenance Fitter.	£6.10.0.	10/-	2.	No.	Elec.
GRAVES, Roland.	- 1	-	-	-	Yes. K.W.		Process Wkr.	£5.15.0.	8/6	2.	No.	Either.
ROSS, James Bernard.	- 1	-	-	-	Yes. K.W.		Driver & Fitter	£5.10.0.		2.	No.	Either.

Appendix Four

APPROVED APPLICANTS.   NONE PRIORITY.   MISCELLANEOUS.

NAMES OF APPLICANTS.	AGES. FAMILY. 4/7 B.G.	8/15 B.G.	15/17 B.G.	Occupation.	Location of Employment. Trad. Bldg. Else. Est. etc. Elsewhere.	Salary or Wages.	Present Rent Paid.	No. of Bedrooms reqd.	Whether Garage Wanted.	Gas or Elec.
SCARLETT, Robert Charles.	-	-	-	Research Off.	Else-where.	£615 p.a.	26/-	3	Not imm.	Gas.
BAKER, David Francis Graham.	-	1	-	Probation Off.	Else-where.	£9. 6.6.	30/-	3.	Not imm.	Gas.
GIBSON, Mitchell.	-	1	-	Pollution & Fishery Off.	Else-where.	£750 p.a.	42/-	3.	Yes.	Gas.
WHITEHOUSE, Maurice Percy.	1	-	-	Technical Rep.	Else-where.	£525 p.a.		3/4	Yes.	Either.
SCULLY, Joseph Wilfred.				Super. Hoover.	Else-where.	£14.0.0.	1o/3	3	Yes.	Elec.
SCOTT, Frank.	1	-	-	Tech. Rep.	Else-where.	£10.0.0.	20/-	3.	Yes.	Either.
CHRISP, Robert Hall.	-	1	-	Super.	Else-where.	£10.0.0.	35/-	3.	Yes.	Either.
GILCHRIST, Alan.	-	1 1 1	-	Com. Trav.	Else-where.	£10.10.0.	15/-	3/4	Yes.	Gas.
BIRKINSHAW, Arthur Turner	-	1 1	-	Sales Rep.	Else-where.	£9.17. 6.	27/-	4	Yes.	Gas.
HILL, Eric.	-	1	-	Service Engr.	Else-where.	£10.0.0.		3.	Yes.	Gas.

Appendix Five

Population growth data for Newton Aycliffe. Before November 1948 the population was essentially a background of approximately 110 people living in the 21 farms and associated cottages.

Documentation on the progress of house construction is based on information from the Newtonian, Development Corporation annual reports and later New Town summary reports to central government as well as the 'Tenants Handbook's. It all began with 41 Prefabs at the end of 1948 and 2 additional houses in Clarence Corner complete in 1949. At the end of 1950 161 houses were complete and 341 at the end of 1951. The Development Corporation then had its own construction department and progress took off apace. The 1000th house was finished in 1953 and the 2000th in 1955. The 3000th house was completed in 1958 and the 4000th in 1962.

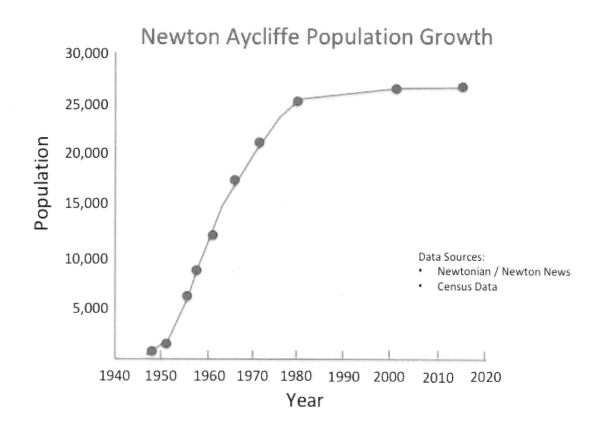

Appendix Six

Memories – a non-scientific compilation of the things that present and former residents of Newton Aycliffe recall doing for recreation and entertainment and that bring back memories of Newton Aycliffe. This information has been compiled from a survey developed on the Facebook page devoted to 'A Photographic History of Newton Aycliffe'. The number of comments totalled about 500 from a group of about 4000+ individuals and some editing has been done to consolidate duplicates etc. Responses are in no particular order and present an overview of what children (largely) enjoyed about life in Newton Aycliffe over the last 75 years.

Carolyn Corner (the first child born in Newton Aycliffe) provided this summary of her experience in 2019 (posted on Facebook and quoted here with her permission):
'I remember living in the Prefab, which is where the baby photo was taken, and going to Sugar Hill School and lots of other random stuff as I lived there until I was 17 when my family moved to Carlbury just outside of Piercebridge. I can remember two men coming to the house to ask my parents if they would allow me to present a bouquet to the Queen and then being bombarded by photographers and reporters. They were everywhere, at home, in school and caught me out walking in the town centre and I was recognised by everyone. I hated it! I was quite shy at 11 and did not like all the attention. I remember shopping for the dress, bought at Fenwicks in Newcastle and going to the dance school to learn how to curtsy and of course the actual event. My father was Ken Corner who was the furniture designer and company director of Toothills until he retired. My mum Lorna Corner, was a very active member of the Town's Women's Guild.'

Generalised Memories of Facebook users:

- The annual Carnival and Fair
- Christmas Eve Santa visit
- Sledging down local hills (the seven hills, Ritson Road, behind the Prefabs etc.)
- Sound of the Town Clock (particularly at night)
- Sound of trains passing on the main line
- Steam trains passing on the Clarence Railway
- Stock car racing at the stadium on the Trading Estate
- Harding's toy shop at the Town Centre
- Collecting newts at various ponds around town
- Boats on the Boating Lake
- Roller-skating, initially at Beveridge Hall and later at St. Oswalds Park. Also on the streets.
- Playing in the Beck (Woodham Burn) – biking, catching tiddlers
- Going brambling on the Trading Estate
- All-nighters at the Youth Club (Northern Soul)
- The 'Meth' – Methodist disco at Neville Parade (often preceded by under age drinking!!)
- Jazz bands
- Pantomime at the Beveridge Hall
- Films on a Saturday morning at the Beveridge Hall
- Trainspotting 'down Ricknall'
- Playing football on the greens – often against teams from other 'greens'
- Tuesday market day
- Really foggy nights
- Ice cream vans – Hooleys, Reas, Mr Whippy
- Visiting pubs – The Dandy Cart, Oak Tree, Iron Horse, Gretna
- The roundabout at the Town Centre – flowers, flag pole
- Rope swings across the Skerne, Woodham Burn etc.
- PG Tips monkeys at the Beveridge Hall
- Going swimming in Darlington, visiting the museum
- Jim's Pies
- The clubs – Workingmen's, Labour, Royal Navy, RAFA, Southerne, British Legion
- Woolworths – particularly inexpensive toys and sweets

- Coffeecana – a 'hipster' hang out for kids in the 1960s

- Company Christmas parties – Bakelite etc.

- Big Chief Fun Week

- Bonfire night – collecting firewood, making the guy, fire in your own back garden

- Driving through Bluebell Woods on The Eden bus

- Potato picking and 'pilfering' turnips to carve Halloween lanterns

- Schools – Sugar Hill, Elmfield, Stephenson Way, Marlowe Hall, Milton Hall, Woodham.

- Factory camaraderie – particularly GEC, UMM, Eatons, Talents, Bakelite, Toothills

- Town Centre when it was 'drive through'

- Making slides in winter

- Renting a tennis court at Simpasture for 50p and keeping it all day if no demand

- Buying sweets at Stevens at Neville Parade

- Christmas trees outside Pryce's at Neville Parade.

- Sonny Steele, who seemed like the town's chief photographer, taking everyone's wedding pictures.